Complete Book of Child Care

AF521584

Published by
Lotus Press Publishers & Distributors

Complete Book of Child Care

Dr. Rajeev Sharma

Lotus Press
4735/22, Prakash Deep Building,
Ansari Road, Daryaganj,
New Delhi - 110002

Lotus Press Publishers & Distributors
Unit No.220, 2nd Floor, 4735/22, Prakash Deep Building,
Ansari Road, Daryaganj, New Delhi- 110002
Ph:- 32903912, 23280047, 098118-38000
Email : lotuspress1984@gmail.com
Visit us : www.lotuspress.co.in

Complete Book of Child Care
© 2015, Dr. Rajeev Sharma
ISBN : 978-81-8382-112-4

All rights reserved. No part of this publication may be reproduced, stored in a retrieval system, or transmitted, in any form or by any means, mechanical, photocopying, recording or otherwise, without prior written permission of the publisher.

Published by : **Lotus Press Publishers & Distributors,** New Delhi- 2
Printed at : **Bharat Offset Works,** New Delhi

PREFACE

Every human being–from birth till puberty–goes through various stages. He masters various skills and abilities while growing. The timing of these stages can act as a guide to parents, reassuring them that all is well if the child is 'on schedule', and giving advance warning of possible difficulties if he is not.

Given the right conditions–the correct food, parental love and understanding–any normal child develops a good moral character and be able to take his place on equal turns with other children.

Ability is inborn, i.e., is inherent. But needs encouragement guidance and love to enhance it. A child starts to react to his environment from the birth.

This book takes a look at all that a child needs while growing up – from nutrition, skin-eye-teeth care to the special care and attention during an illness. Emotional and psychological problems as well as teaching a child the valuable lessons in good manners are also dealt with. The book also covers issues on immunisation and first aid. This book is intended for mothers and would-be-mothers who can take guidance in bringing up their children.

There are seperate chapters on Treatment Through Ayurveda, Homoeopathy, Complimentary Therapies and General Caution on Administration of medicines.

Astrological Guide for Child and Chart of Common Problems and infections Illnesses will certainly be helpful to all the readers. I am thankful to Dr. Sudhir Gehalot, M.D. Neonatologist and Paediatrician for his sincere advises.

–Dr. Rajeev Sharma

e-mail: sharmarajeev108@rediffmail.com

CONTENTS

1

FROM PREGNANCY TO CHILDBIRTH

All the information for making a new human being are contained in the male and female sex cells. When these cells meet at the right time and place, they fuse to form a single new cell, which is smaller than a dot. From such a scrap of tissue, a complete human life emerges.

Inherited characteristics, such as the colour of the eyes and the hair, body structure and mental ability, are passed on from the parents to the baby by thousands of complex chemical substances called genes. These are all contained in the original fertilised egg. In ordinary body cells, the genes are lined up along microscopic rod-shaped chromosomes in the central part of every cell. There are 23 pairs or 46 chromosomes in each body cell, the male and female sex cells have 23 pairs each. When the sex cells unite in the woman's body at fertilisation, the new cell is formed – which eventually develops into a baby – contains the full complement of 46 chromosomes.

Of the 23 pairs of chromosomes in human body cells, 22 pairs are identical to each other. The 23rd pairs is the sex chromosomes, called X and Y, which are their shapes as seen through a microscope. Females have two X-chromosomes, so the combination XX is female. All human eggs–'half cells' formed by the splitting of normal cells in a woman's ovaries–must, therefore, contain one X-chromosome.

Males on the other hand, have one X-chromosome and one Y-chromosome in their body cells, and the combination XY is male. As a result, sperms, also consisting of 'half cells', contain either an X-chromosome or a Y-chromosome, half the sperms are X and half are Y. At conception, a sperm and an egg fuse to form a single full cell which develops into an embryo and eventually into a new human being.

The sex of the baby depends on the type of sperm – X or Y – which fertilises the egg; a sperm carrying an X-chromosome results a girl, and sperm with a Y-chromosome results in a boy.

Development of the Baby

As a fertilised egg passes down the fallopian tube it divides, so that by the time it reaches the womb it already consists of a ball of cells, called a blastocyst. This then sinks into the lining of the womb and continues to grow. Soon the outer layer of the blastocyst forms the placenta, a disc-shaped connection between the growing embryo and the mother.

Within the thickness of the placenta, blood vessels from the embryo form branching projections, which are surrounded by blood from the mother's blood circulation. The two bloodstreams remain separate and do not mingle. Oxygen, carbon dioxide, nutrients and waste products can pass freely from one circulation to the other – as can germs of infections such as syphilis and rubella.

As the embryo grows in size, it becomes separated from the other tissues derived from the blastocyst. The embryo lies in a fluid-filled sac, called the amniotic cavity, enclosed by two membranes, the amnion and the chorion.

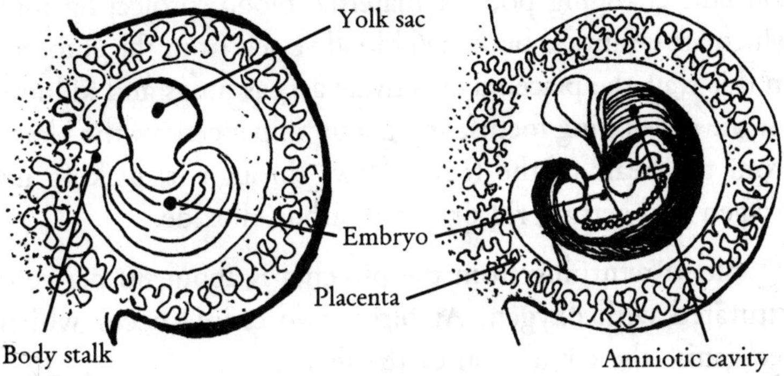

The umbilical cord, containing two arteries and one vein, connects the embryo to the placenta. The blood flows from the foetus to the placenta in the umbilical arteries, and returns via the umbilical veins.

How the Baby Grows in the Womb

By the fourth week of pregnancy, the embryo is about the size of a pigeon's egg, and has blood cells and primitive circulation, although the heart has not yet developed. Within the second month or eighth week of pregnancy, the embryo grows to about the size of a hen's egg, and the foetus has a recognizably human form and all the major organs and limbs have formed.

At 12 weeks, the foetus is nearly 3 inches long, 5 inches at 16 weeks, 10 inches at 20 weeks, and 18 inches at

36 weeks. At birth the average length of a baby is about 20 inches, and the weight averages between two and a half to three and a half kilogrammes.

Nourishment for the Baby

The growth of the embryo depends on nutrients supplied from the mother's bloodstream. The placenta provides a constant changing pool of maternal blood, projecting into which are countless branched blood vessels from the embryo. In this way, the placenta effectively acts as lungs and kidneys for the developing foetus, and about 55 per cent of the blood from the heart of the foetus flows through it, picking up oxygen and getting rid of waste carbon dioxide.

Blood returning from the placenta is about 80 per cent saturated with oxygen. At birth, two events occur which reorganise the circulation of the foetus.

Blood stops flowing through the placenta as it is compressed in the otherwise empty womb; and the gasping of the newborn baby – deprived of the supply of oxygenated blood from the placenta – causes the lungs to expand. The pressure rises in the circulation to the left side of the heart and falls on the right. The opening in the centre partition of the heart (which has been diverting blood from right to left) is closed by a flap forced shut by the rise in pressure in the left side.

Shortly afterwards the other bypass, the ductus arteriosus, also closes. The two sides of the heart are now separate units. Many forms of congenital heart disease are due to failure of a heart openings to close. The condition is known as hole in the heart. Some infants with heart defects have dusky complexion, and are called blue babies.

The Mother during Pregnancy

The average term of pregnancy is 273 days, calculated from the day on which conception took place. Usually, however, pregnancy is dated from the first day of the last normal menstrual period. To calculate the expected date of delivery, 280 days are added to this date.

Shortly after the first missed period other symptoms begin. The breasts increase in size, become slightly tender and later the skin darken around the nipples. Morning sickness may start from the sixth week, and often persists for two to three months. At about the second month, the expectant mother may wants to pass urine more frequently, because the enlarging womb compresses her bladder.

During pregnancy, the mother gains about 11 kgs in weight. The volume of her blood rises by a quarter, and her skin becomes darker and greasier, although in some the complexion improves. The normal loss of hair from the scalp stops.

The steady increase in the size of the womb leads to changes in postures. Less room in the abdomen leads to some indigestion, possibly to constipation. Sometimes the rise in pressure inside the abdomen causes varicose veins and haemorrhoids.

A pregnant woman needs more nourishing food, and her appetite generally improves. The baby needs iron and calcium for its growth, therefore the mother should supplement her diet with more iron and calcium. Most expectant mothers are given tablets containing iron and folic acid to prevent any deficiencies.

Early in pregnancy, the mother should guard against overeating and putting on too much weight. Protein-rich foods should be eaten rather than starchy carbohydrates. Fats from the dairy products are useful as an aid to an adequate intake of vitamins; and milk should be drunk for its calcium content. Iron can be obtained from lean red meat, liver and leafy green vegetables such as spinach.

A woman should remain active all through her pregnancy. Labour requires considerable physical effort, and she needs to be physically fit. Regular walking in the fresh air and routine housework help, but violent exercise should be avoided.

A pregnant woman's daily diet should contain at least 4 cups of milk, 2 or more fruits (one yellow or deep green ones), one or more eggs, 6-8 chapatis, 3 to 4 servings of rice or bread, 4 tablespoon of oil or ghee, and 250 grammes or more of meat, fish, poultry or a bowl of dal. At least 8 glasses of water every day needs to be taken.

Problems of Pregnancy

Morning sickness–a feeling of nausea and actual vomiting on waking up–is very common in the early weeks of pregnancy. Usually the expectant mother feels quite well for the rest of the day, and simple treatment with glucose drinks on waking is all that is required. In severe cases, the doctors may prescribe a long-acting antihistamine drug to prevent nausea which can be taken at bed-time; it is still effective in the morning.

Excessive vomiting throughout the day, known as hyperemesis gravidarum, is a serious problem, and if it does not respond to simple drug treatment, a stay in hospital may be needed. Almost invariably the vomiting stops within hours of admission suggesting that the condition has a psychological element.

Many pregnant women find they have a strong craving for unusual foods–like apples, bananas, or even an inedible substance such as coal. One theory is that this craving is due to a deficiency of iron, and treatment with iron tablets is usually effective.

Heartburn is a common problem, and is caused when swelling of the abdomen alters the angle at which the oesophagus enters the stomach. As with other problems of pregnancy that are caused by physical factors, the treatment is limited to relieving the symptoms. This is done by giving antacid preparations, and by advising the patient to sleep propped up in bed.

Varicose veins and haemorrhoids are also the result of the mechanical stresses of pregnancy and commonly cease once the baby is born. Bandaging of the legs and periods or rest in the afternoon ease varicose veins. Constipation aggravates haemorrhoids, and should be prevented by a diet rich in fresh fruits and vegetables.

Toxaemia of pregnancy is a condition of unknown cause affecting the kidneys where the body retains salt and water instead of eliminating them through the urine. It is more common in women expecting their first baby. Untreated toxaemia (also known as pre-eclampsia), can lead to the dangerous condition of eclampsia, in which a series of convulsions is followed by premature labour.

Without exception, eclampsia can be prevented by proper treatment of toxaemia. One of the main purposes of antenatal care is the detection of early signs of toxaemia – swelling of the ankles, traces of protein in the urine, slight rises of blood pressure, or excess gain in weight. Even if the expectant mother feels perfectly fit, she should have regular medical checks. Mild toxaemia is treated simply by rest; occasionally a stay in hospital may be required. Drug treatment with sedatives and hypotensive drugs may also be needed in a few cases.

Rhesus mismatch may arise during pregnancy in a woman with rhesus negative blood who is married to a man that has rhesus positive blood. In the past, she ran the risk of having her babies affected by a blood disorder. Antibodies formed in the mother's body against the rhesus factor present in the blood cells of a rhesus positive baby cause this condition. But today rhesus negative women can be reassured that this condition can be prevented. Rhesus disease develops after rhesus positive blood enters the circulation of a rhesus negative woman: a mismatched blood transfusion, an abortion, or the birth of a rhesus positive baby. If a special antibody is given to the woman within a few hours of any of these events, no reaction occurs.

An attack of rubella (German measles) in the second or third month of pregnancy may cause deformities in the unborn baby, including deafness, blindness and heart disease. For this reason, most doctors regard such an illness as medical grounds for an abortion. The problem should become less common with the increasing use of rubella vaccine.

After the first six weeks or so of pregnancy, warning signs of a possible abortion are bleeding from the vagina and colicky pain in the lower abdomen. Rest in bed for a few days may preserve the pregnancy; but if the embryo has died the abortion is inevitable.

Repeated miscarriages may be caused by a defect in the womb or because the hormones are not functioning properly; in many cases there is no obvious cause. Treatment is usually a combination of rest in early pregnancy combined with drug treatment. Physical defects can sometimes be corrected surgically.

The Birth of the Baby

By the ninth month of pregnancy, the baby is usually lying upside-down in the womb. The head sinks down firmly into the mother's pelvis, ready for birth. In the first stage of labour, which lasts about nine hours, the muscular walls of the womb contract, pressing the head of the baby against the cervix.

As contractions continue, the pressure of the head of the baby slowly stretches the cervix open. These contractions grow longer and more intense. At the end of the first stage, the cervix opens. The amniotic sac breaks, releasing fluid. This is 'the breaking of the waters'. The head is forced into the vagina. Once it passes between the bones surrounding the birth canal, the mother is generally told to bear down to push the baby outwards.

In the second stage of labour, which lasts for an hour to two hours, the baby is born. As it leaves the birth canal, its head faces the mother's back. Her backbone is forced down to let the baby pass. After the head of the baby has emerged, the shoulders, which are turned, slip out easily. The rest of the body is quickly delivered–with the baby's first cry, breathing begins. The umbilical cord is cut.

In the final stage of labour the womb discharges the placenta and the remains of the umbilical cord, which are forced out through the vagina. The womb returns to normal size about 10 days after birth.

If the second stage is delayed, the doctor may use forceps or a vacuum extractor to ease the baby out. In some cases the doctor performs an episiotomy, a simple operation to increase the size of the opening of the birth canal and thus prevent any tearing of the skin or muscle. This incision, in the skin at the side of the vagina, is sewn up immediately after delivery of the baby.

Sometimes the baby does not lie in the womb in such a way that it can be born head first. Breech presentation is the medical term for being born bottom first, and it may require skilful management by the attendant obstetrician.

2

CARE OF THE NEW BORN BABY

After the baby is born, he or she adjusts rapidly to the new surroundings in the hospital. The baby no longer gets oxygen from the mother's blood, and this lack of oxygen stimulates the respiratory centre in the baby's brain, and he begins to breathe.

The hospital staff shows him to his mother before taking him away for cleaning. The nurse takes the baby's temperature, records his weight, time of birth, and measures his length. She examines his head, ears, arms, hands, fingers, feet, legs and toes. Any obvious defects are detected at this time.

After cleaning the baby, the nurse trims the umbilical cord with sterile scissors.

The Mother after Birth

Many mothers wish to breast-feed the baby, and this should be started as early as possible after the birth. For the first few days, the mother's breasts secrete a yellow substance, colostrum, which is rich in antibodies, contain less sugar and more minerals than milk. Within four days colostrum is replaced by milk.

The stimulus to formation of milk by the breasts is sucking by the baby. Baby, if healthy, should be demand fed.

Exertion should be limited for 14 days or so after the birth, but the mother should be out of bed for short periods on the third day. Depending on her state of health, the mother can leave the hospital after the third day.

A newborn baby hardly resembles the chubby, cuddlesome babies that you see in advertisements. He is covered with a waxy material, which vanishes after a couple of days. His skin underneath is very red, the face appears puffy and lumpy, and there may be blue and black marks left by forceps. Some babies have bluish marks around the hips that gradually disappear, as they grow older.

Some parents worry about the size of a newborn baby's head, which seems too large and heavy for the neck to support it. But this is normal. Most have an oddly shaped head at first, prominent in some places, flat in others, but this is only due to the stress exerted during labour. This is temporary, and within a few days, will return to its normal round shape. It is normal for a baby to lie where he is put – he cannot, at first, roll over or change his position. Hence it is desirable to change his sleeping position so that he gets uniform pressure on all sides of the head.

In some babies, the colour of the skin tinges to a slight yellow 48 hours after birth, and usually disappears within 3-4 days. This is due to the liver, which has not yet fully matured. If the colour deepens and goes on increasing, then the doctor should be notified immediately before it can prove fatal.

A newborn baby cannot adjust his body temperature to suit variations in the temperature around him. It is therefore important to keep him in a fairly even temperature at first, or to make sure that he has clothing or bedding to protect him when it is cold. But do not overdress the baby; too many clothes may be uncomfortable; remember that a reasonably plump baby needs less covering than an adult. The best way of deciding whether or not the baby is cold is to feel his hands and feet. Do not put a newborn baby out of doors in frosty or foggy weather; no amount of wrapping up can protect his lungs against the cold air he will breathe.

A newborn baby has limited resistance to infection: if you have a cold avoid passing on your infection when handling him, by covering your nose and mouth with a large handkerchief tied behind the head. Although the mother will be mainly responsible for looking after the baby, it is important that the father should also help right from the beginning. In this way, the child develops an understanding that both parents are of equal importance; it also gives the mother a rest if the father takes his turn to bathe the baby. As long as your baby feeds well, sleeps well and gains weight evenly, there is nothing to worry about.

Bathing a Baby

Bathing should be fun for both mother and the baby, so organise bath-time to allow opportunity for the child to splash and play about in the water. Have everything ready and within reach before you start. Do not attempt to clean the baby's ears; and if his nose is clogged with mucus, clean it with a twisted cotton wool (not with cotton wool on a wooden stick). *Never leave a baby alone in a bath.* Swich off the fan before bathing the baby.

Put cold water in bath, then hot. Test it with your elbow; it should be comfortably warm. Lay the baby on your lap. Wash his face with water only. Wash baby's hair with a little soap. Use a flannel or sponge to wet and rinse. Wet and soap baby's body, neck, arms and legs, using your hands or the flannel.

Lift the baby, supporting his head on your wrist and arm, put the baby in the bath. Keeping his head supported, rinse off the soap. Gently splash a little water on to the baby's body. Lay baby on a towel on your lap. Dry him thoroughly, and sprinkle with baby powder.

Putting on a Nappy

There are three methods of folding a nappy: triangle, kite and rectangular (see the figures on next page). The method you choose depends largely upon your baby's size, for the nappy must not bunch so much between his legs that it keeps them widely apart. Nor should the nappy fit too tightly – just tight enough to keep it comfortably in place. Always slip your fingers between the nappy and the baby for protection before fixing a nappy pin.

Triangle Method

Take a square piece of soft, sturdy cloth. Fold the nappy corner to corner to make a double thick triangle. Lay the baby on the nappy with his legs towards the pointed side and his waist at the centre/wide side. Fold the sides of the triangle over the baby's stomach so that they overlap. Pass the third corner lying between his bottoms up his legs to meet the other two corners. Pin the corners together with a single pin, taking care to protect the baby from being pricked.

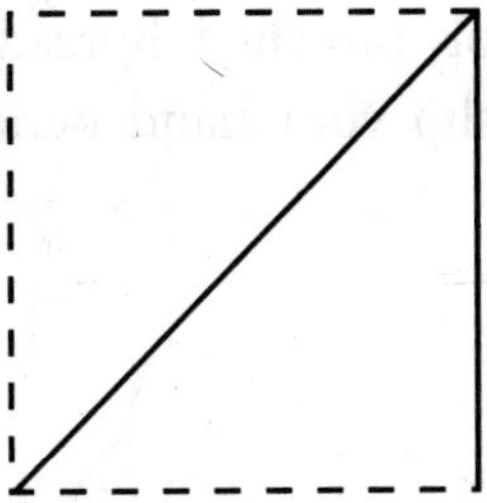

Kite Method

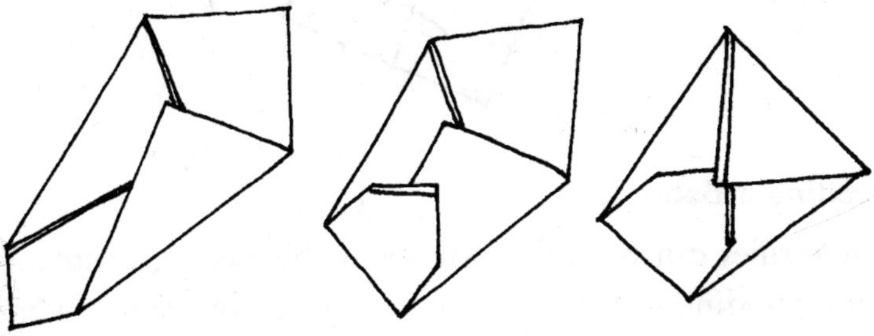

Fold one corner from halfway along one side and about three-quarters along the other. Repeat with the opposite corner. Lay the baby on the nappy with his legs towards the shortest fold of shape, and his waist on the opposite fold. Lift one corner over the baby's body, take the nappy up between his legs and pin together. Lift the other corner over his body and underneath the rest of the nappy. Pin the folds together. The fitted nappy should be just enough to stay in place without slipping.

Rectangular Method

Fold the nappy in two to form an oblong, and then fold over one-third of it. Place the baby with his waist about level with the top of the thicker part of the folded nappy. Fold the thinner part of the nappy up between his legs, making sure it is not uncomfortably bunched. Spread the folded part over the baby's tummy, slip your hand beneath the nappy, and pin it.

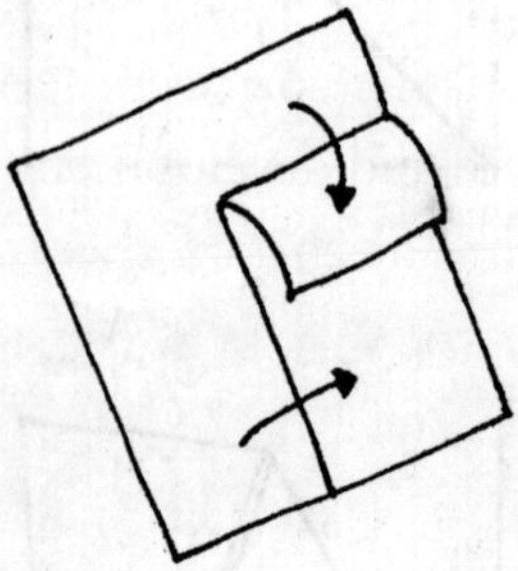

Feeding a Baby

Some rules can be laid down about the feeding of infants. Breast-feeding goes in and out of fashion for reasons which are not always medical; but there is no doubt that breast milk is ideal for a baby's nutrition–and it is supplied at exactly the correct temperature.

In the first few weeks of life, breast-fed babies are less likely to get stomach disorders than bottle-fed babies. This is because breast milk is almost germ free. It contains antibodies against some infections, and when it reaches the baby's intestines it is more resistant to the growth of bacteria than is cow's milk.

Bottle-feeding is medically necessary only when a mother is unable to supply enough breast milk or the baby will not accept the nipple. A baby thrives perfectly well on a bottle as long as you observe strict cleanliness, and make sure the hole in the teat is right (large, medium or small), and the formula is mixed correctly.

It is extremely important that teats and bottles should be clean: wash them with soapy water immediately after use, then sterilise them with boiling water or a cold water sterilising agent.

Breast milk contains the correct proportions of nutrients necessary for the growth and development of the baby. When the baby starts sucking at the mother's breast, the breast stimulation produces milk, which is a happy experience both for the mother and the baby, giving them emotional satisfaction.

Breast milk has several more nutrients than cow's milk or other formula. Since it is readily available and free of cost, it is the ultimate convenient food. It has a healthy dose of antibodies that increases immunity to diseases. There is less stress on the baby's kidneys as the breast milk is low in sodium and protein. Similarly, low levels of phosphorus help the baby absorb calcium better. They find the milk easy to digest, and hence have less chances of suffering from colic and gas. The close contact between mother and child during breast-feeding creates a special bond between them.

The mother stands to gain when she breast-feeds her baby. It helps to bring her uterus to the pre-pregnancy size, that is, it shrinks. She is able to burn about 500 kilo calories or more in a day, and this helps her in shedding the extra weight gained during pregnancy. She has less risks of pregnancy during the period she breast-feeds as ovulation and menstruation are suppressed. She has less risk of developing breast cancer occurring at an earlier stage. She gets a much-needed rest while feeding her baby.

The mother should ensure absolute cleanliness while breast-feeding. Before nursing the baby, she should wash her hands with soap and water, and ensure that her hands are not very cold. The nipples must be washed with warm water. It would be advisable to feed for short periods only in the first 3-4 days, as the amount of colostrum secreted is less.

Once regular breast-feeding starts, she must nurse the baby for about 10 minutes on either breast. It is important to use both breasts for feeding.

Feeding on demand when the baby cries is not necessarily the correct method for every mother and baby, nor is regular feeding by the clock (every four hours, in the first weeks of life) necessarily the best. A strict timetable may suit one baby, whereas a free and easy approach to feeding may suit another mother and child.

3

EQUIPMENT AND CLOTHES FOR INFANTS

A newborn baby needs some basic, but essential, equipment to make him comfortable. The essential items need to be purchased before the baby is born. These include clothes, blankets, sheets, nappies, bath items, pram, weighing scale, and feeding paraphernalia. He also needs a comfortable place to sleep in.

Baby's Crib

This can be of metal, wood or cane, or you can use a collapsible one, which eliminates space problem. Use a firm mattress and cover it with a very soft sheet. You can use soft bolsters on either side of the baby to keep him snug and warm. Spread a waterproof or rubber sheet between the mattress and cotton sheet.

You will need another smaller waterproof sheet covered with a small cotton cover, when you want to carry the baby for feeding.

Toddler's Bed

To help your child to make switch to a big bed, recreate a secure environment like the one he had in his cot or cradle.

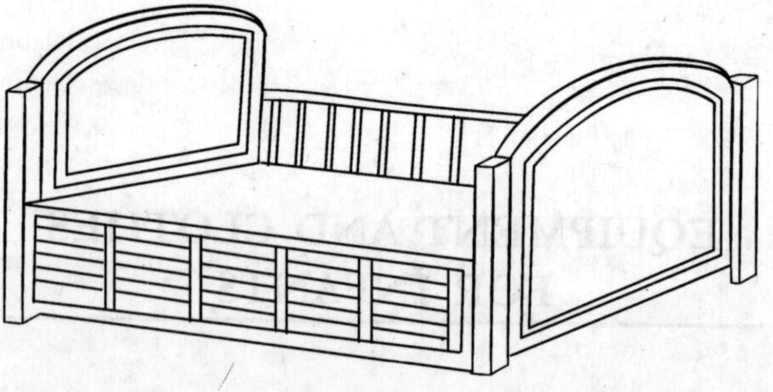

You can start convincing him that he is now a big boy, and how fortunate he is to sleep in a big bed "like mummy and daddy do". You can spread his toys around his pillow, and keep a dim light burning in his room.

The toddler too needs a hard mattress with a soft, thin pillow for his head. He still needs a rubber sheet in his bed as a precautionary measure against bed-wetting. You can place a few pillows or cushions around him to give him a feeling of being snug and secure, and also to avoid his falling off the bed.

Blankets

Babies should have two to three blankets, preferably made from light flannel. These are easy to handle and wash. You can purchase a bright, flannel cloth, cut it to the desired size and have piping made of satin. If the flannel is plain and not printed, you can either stitch motifs on all corners or paint small flowers or cartoon characters. For the cold winter, you can have light woollen blankets. For older infants also, such blankets come in handy. But they now need bigger sized ones.

Clothes and Dresses

Baby's clothes should be loose to allow free movement. Cotton fabric would be ideal material and in warm conditions, thin and soft materials like voile or muslin would be preferable. In summer you can have just a vest for the baby, with velcro for fastening the lapels together, instead of using buttons or zips.

Avoid using panties for the baby as this may result in rashes on the thigh. Use diapers made of light and soft cotton. It would be cheaper to use homemade diapers rather than purchase the ready-made ones, which can be used if you are taking the baby out.

In winter babies should be warmly wrapped up in woollen clothes. Over a cotton vest, you can use a light woollen sweater that is loose, and buttons up in the front. They can wear light woollen socks and mitts, but see that there is no elastic in them. You can have brightly coloured satin ribbons to fasten them, but ensure that after tying the ribbons, the socks and mitts are not too tight for the babies.

As your baby grows up to be a toddler, he will develop the coordination to dress himself successfully. As he becomes more involved in dressing himself, he will become more conscious of the clothes he wears, unlike babies who do not know what they are wearing as long as they are warm and comfortable. Toddlers are by now noticing colours and the type of clothing they put on. Your child may have a fancy for a particular outfit. It could be because he feels very comfortable in it, or else its colour, or the feel of the garment attracts him.

Allowing your child to choose which clothes to wear each day is also important. He may develop an irrational dislike for certain items of clothing. The easiest way to handle such a situation is to go along with these preferences as far as feasible, although occasionally, when you are going out, you would like to see him dressed up in the newer clothes instead of the faded or frayed clothes that he is fond of.

Until your child has enough dexterity to manage the cumbersome buttons and zips, you need to choose clothes and shoes with manageable fastenings. Help him to dress himself to allow him independence, and do not step in to help unless you are really needed, or he requests you.

Trousers with elasticized waists are the easiest but if he has trousers with zip fasteners, show him how to pull the zip away from him as he closes it to prevent it catching. It would be easier for him to handle the zip if it has a ring attached to the tab. If he wears dungarees, look for buttons or adjustable straps so that the straps can be adjusted.

If your toddler is a girl, she will try to dress herself now. So choose clothes that she can manage without any hassles. Do not invest too much on her clothes as she is growing up quickly and will soon outgrow her clothes.

Choose dresses with fastenings at the front; those at the back will be too difficult for the kid to manage all by herself. It is best to have loose clothes to allow much room for growth. Choose clothes that are bright, but not garish.

At 18 months your toddler will be trying to manage fastenings, and by two and a half years he or she will be able to close button in a loose buttonhole and put on the pants, T-shirt and sweatshirt, or frock or skirt and blouse. By the age of four he will probably be able to dress or undress himself completely and may be able to put away his clothes tidily.

You can teach her or him how to button from the bottom upwards. It would be easy for the children to have velcro fastenings, as they are easy to manage. When wearing sweaters they should be taught that the label always goes at the back, for they have a tendency to put them on the wrong way round.

Choosing Shoes

While shopping for your child's shoes, allow the assistant to measure the length and width of your child's foot before your child tries any shoes. Once he tries them on, press on the joints of the foot to make sure that they are not constricting in any way. Once the fastenings have been done, ensure that your child's foot does not slip out or too tight. Make him walk up and down to check that he is comfortable in them.

It should be sturdy, preferably made of leather that is suitable for general outdoor wear, especially once your child goes out to play. A pair of sports shoes would also do for playing outdoors. sports shoes can also be worn, so long as they fit your child's feet well. Velcro fastenings rather than laces or buckles will allow your child to fasten his own shoes very easily.

Bathing Necessities

For a baby you need a bathtub made of solid, durable plastic. Buy mild soap, shampoo, cream, lotion, oil, and talc—all products specially made for babies. Have soft cotton buds for cleaning ears and nose superficially. Never insert them deeply. Then you need a body towel for the baby and one for yourself when you remove the baby from the tub on to your lap.

For toddlers, baths should be carefully supervised, for he is at risk from slipping and falling under the water in the bathtub. Hence, place a non-slip bath mat in the bottom of the bath. He too needs a towel, made of soft cotton, to wipe his body. Mild soap and shampoo are good for him. If he likes to play in the tub for some time, he can be allowed to have some rubber toys with him in the bath.

Choosing a Pram

One of the most important points in choosing a pram is to make sure that the hood, when raised, should not be so high that it obscures your view of the path ahead. Ideally, its highest point should be just below shoulder level. The handle of the pram should be at elbow level, so that the forearm is parallel with the ground when pushing the pram, and there is no strain on your back.

A baby should be confined by baby straps, and have a pillow to support his back. Parcels and shopping items are best carried beneath the pram body, between the wheels. A day out with the baby, when the weather is pleasant, gives the baby some essential exposure to the sun, plus some fresh air.

If the toddler is tired, and cannot walk far, it is easier to push him in a pram, rather than carry him, especially when you have to carry shopping items.

Feeding Equipment

For the baby, you need 3-4 feeding bottles for water, juice, etc. At the time of weaning, he will need a spill-proofer sipper or baby tumbler. You need a good bottlebrush for cleaning the bottles, and a large pan for sterilising the bottles.

You can use either porcelain or a plastic cup to mix cereals in, and a stainless steel spoon for mixing it.

Older infants will need a bowl, made of plastic or stainless steel, with a spoon. They can have a beautifully coloured plate in case they have a variety of food to eat, especially *bread* or *chapati*. They can have smaller cups in plastic or stainless steel for *dal* or *soup* or vegetables or even curd. They can use portable chairs that can be fixed to your dining table. He will definitely need a bib to protect his clothes.

Weighing Scales

To keep a record of your baby or child's weight, it is essential that you have weighing scales at home. Weigh yourself with the baby, and then weigh yourself. The difference in the weights will be your baby's weight. A toddler can easily stand on the scale, so you will have no problem checking his weight.

4

IMPORTANT MILESTONES

Here are some tabels regarding over all growth of child at diffrent months.

Caution: The age of attainment of a milestone is a gross average. If a child achieves a milestone before, it doesn't mean that he will be more advanced than other children and vice-versa. For example, a child may walk at 10 months, while another may walk at 18 months, even though both are normal. However if your child doesn't attain a particular milestone within the specified period, consult your doctor. In most of the cases, it will turn out to be a normal variant only. Parents can make a serial record in the column 'age achieved' below.

CROSS MOTOR

	Milestone	Achievement age (for parental recording)
1.	Neck control	4 months
2.	Roll (Front to back, and vice-versa)	5-6 months
3.	Sits	6-7 months
4.	Crawls/Creeps	9-10 months

5. Stands and Walks	12-16 months
6. Runs	2 years
7. Up and Down Stairs	3 years
8. Rides Tricycle	3 years
9. Hops on one foot	4 year
10. Skips Rope	5-6 years

FINE MOTOR

Milestone	Achievement age (for parental recording)
1. Hands Predominantly Open	3 months
2. Hands Grasp Objects /Hand Regard	4 months
3. Foot Play	5 months
4. Transfers Objects from Hand to Hand	6 months
5. Ulnar (Towards Little Finger) Grasp	5-6 months
6. Radial (Towards Thumb) Grasp	8-10 months
7. Index Finger Approach to Objects	10 months
8. Good Use of Cup and Spoon	18 months
9. Horizontal/Vertical Stroke with Pen	2 years
10. Undress and Dresses Self	3 years

SOCIAL AND COGNITIVE

Milestone	Achievement age (for parental recording)
1. Smiles on Social Interaction	1 - 2 months
2. Recognises Mother	3 months
3. Show Emotions (Anger, Fear etc.)	4 months
4. Smiles at Image in Mirror	5 months

5. Object Permanence	7-8 months
6. Separation Anxiety	6-12 months
7. Waves bye-bye; Responds to Name	10 months
8. Autonomy (Struggle with Parents)	1½ years
9. Narrates Immediate Expereinces	2 years
10. Knows Age, Sex and Name	3 years

PLAY

Milestone	Achievement age (for parental recording)
1. Plays "Peek-a'Boo", "Pat-a-Cake"	10 months
2. Mimicry and Imitation of Others	12 months
3. Rolling Ball, Gathering Ball	15-18 months
4. "Pretend" Play with Doll	2-5 years
5. Parallel Play (Imitates Other's Play)	2-3 years
6. Co-operative Play (Takes Part)	3-4 years

SPEECH AND LANGUAGE

Milestone	Achievement age (for parental recording)
1. Coos i.e. Vocalises	2 months
2. Says "Aati", "Cnah". Enjoy Music	3 months
3. Monosyllabic Babble (Pa, Da, Ma)	6 months
4. Polosyllabic Babble (Ba-Da-Ma, Mama)	8 - 10 months
5. Follows / Obeys 1 Step Command	10 months
6. First Real, Meaningful Word	12 months
7. Points out to Major Body Parts	15 months
8. 10-15 Words Vocabulary	18 months
9. Forms Sentence, 100 Word Vocabulary	2 years
10. Follows /Obey 2 Step Commands	2 years

5

BREAST FEEDING SPECIAL

Breast feeding can be started after delivery as soon as both the mother and the baby are comfortable (particularly when the baby starts moving his head about with movement of his lips as if he is trying to 'search' for the nipple). Correct position and technique are necessary for optimal sucking with minimal nipple discomfort.

If the mother is siting, the infant should be elevated to the height of the breast and turned so that he faces the mother and their abdomens touch. The mother's arm supporting the baby should bring the baby's mouth in line with her breast and near to it. The other free arm should support the breast from below by her fingers, while the thumb and the index finger should grasp the nipple and compress it so to make it more protractile. The infant's initial licking and mouthing helps the nipple in being more erect. Ideally, the mother should touch the nipple at the corner of the baby's mouth and not directly stick it into the baby's mouth. When the baby feels the nipple (or any stimulus including a finger touch at the corner of his mouth), he goes for it, depending upon his hunger. The baby tries to 'catch' the stimulus (in this case the nipple) in his mouth, a natural reflex called rooting. When the baby, with its mouth open finds the nipple and tries to grasp it, the mother should gently but rapidly, push as much nipple and areola as possible in the baby's mouth.

The baby would apply rhythmic compressions on the areola (and not on the nipple, as it does in bottle-feeding) with its gums. Milk is stored in sinuses underneath the areola and these sinuses should be compressed rhythmically, so that the milk from them is squired via the nipple into the baby's mouth. The nipple acts like a conduit for the passage of milk. Chewing on the nipple or rhythmic compression of the nipple by the gums is not helpful in getting the milk, because milk from the breast doesn't come from suction on the nipples as in case of bottle! Proper breast feeding technique requires that the baby compresses the areola (rather than the nipples) with it gums. In fact, improper technique and positioning is chiefly responsible for soreness and cracked nipples (a common complaint of nursing mothers).

Some useful advice regarding breast-feeding are given below:

- Express some milk from the sinuses before feeding. It makes the areolar area soft and compressible for the baby.
- Both breasts should be offered to the baby at one feed. The breast offered first should be completely emptied (emptying is a potent stimulus for milk production).
- The breast to be offered first should be alternated with feeds, i.e. if the left breast was offered first during the previous feed the right should be offered first now. This ensures complete emptying of at least one breast at each

feeding, which is very necessary for adequate milk production.

The optimal period for sucking at each breast is about 15 minutes after the 3rd day. On the 1st day, it is 5 minutes and on the 2nd, 10 minutes. However, it depends more on the baby. Some babies finish their milk requirements fast in just 3-4 minutes and then doze off. Others may do it at a leisurely pace. However, suckling for more than 15 minutes is not advocated as it may lead to soreness and cracked nipples, plus the baby takes his milk during that time.

When the baby has finished feeding, don't pull it away from your breast. It will apply traction on the nipple and may make it sore. The best way to unlatch a baby is to insert your finger in the corner of baby's mouth in between the gums. This will release the grasp of the gums and then you can take the baby off the breast.

If the baby dozes off while feeding, you can gently stimulate the baby by massaging behind the ears or rubbing the soles of the baby. If after 2-3 tries, the baby is still not feeding, then stop and unlatch the baby.

There is no fixed time interval (say 3 hours or 4 hours) at which the baby has to be fed. Instead a flexible schedule is recommended based chiefly on demand; i.e. to give the baby the milk when he starts demanding it. But if more than 4 hours elapse and the baby is still sleepy, it is better to try to awaken him gently and see whether he will accept feeds.

The milk produced in the initial 3-4 days is fluidly, yellow and very less in amount. It is called 'colostrum', which has a high content of nutrients and is invaluable to the child. It should always be given to the baby, without worrying about its quality.

During this phase, the mother starts doubting that she is not producing enough milk. All mothers produce colostrum (which as I have mentioned is physiologically less in amount) and all of them produce roughly the same amount in the initial 2-3 days. By the 4th of day, the milk production starts increasing and adjusts itself to the baby's needs in another few days.

It is during this time that the mother turns towards the bottle to supplement her 'inadequate' breast milk (which is actually adequate for the baby). The baby's fluid and calorie requirements are less during the first 1-3 days, and so the 'less' amount of milk is actually sufficient This is the critical point where all the trouble starts. Once the baby starts accepting the bottle feed the motivation of mother goes down. The baby finding the nipple of the bottle softer than the breast has to put less efforts to derive milk from it, and so starts preferring it over the breast. It appears that all human beings including a one-day old seek the easy way out. The mother on seeing the baby prefer the bottle becomes so discouraged that it becomes very difficult for her to breast-feed. Then there is an entity called 'nipple confusion'. The baby's gum compresses the areola of the mother rather than the nipple, but with the bottle the baby compresses rhythmically the bottle's nipple. This may lead to confusion in the baby's mind and he may start chewing on the nipples of the mother's breasts, and on finding no milk coming may become irritated. Therefore, if you want to breast-feed, no bottles, even for some feeds, until you are confident and have a well-established milk supply.

A very important prerequisite for a nursing mother is that she should be mentally and physically relaxed. Tension and fatigue has an inhibitory effect on milk production. After delivery don't encourage long visits by well wishers. Instead try to rest sleep or just relax with your baby by the side, thinking pleasurable thoughts about it.

The breast-feeding mother should consume adequate amounts of water and a wholesome diet. Wholesome diet doesn't mean eating lots of fattening things like *ghee*, chocolates, cakes etc. but to eat cereals, pulses, vegetables, eggs, meat, curd etc. Eating lot of fruits is a good thing. Drinking a lot of milk in the belief that it will indirectly 'come out' from the breasts and so replace the milk taken by the baby is an erroneous belief. By all means drink milk (and lots of it), if you really relish it. But drinking if for the reason mentioned above (while you inner self doesn't really want to) is not recommended.

As discussed earlier in detail, there is a fine-tuning by nature between the production of milk and its demand by thc baby. The amount of milk produced is not a 'static' quantity e.g. one mother may produce 500 cc per day while another may produce 700 cc per day. Milk production increases according to the baby's requirements. If the baby wants more, it sucks more, which empties the breast completely. This is the most potent stimulus to produce more milk. So more the demand, more is the supply.

6

NUTRITION FOR INFANTS

A growing child needs a well-balanced diet to provide all the calories, vitamins and minerals he needs. There should be plenty of calcium to build strong teeth and bones. Cheese, milk and fish are good sources. Vitamin D, found in oily fish, eggs and butter, is also necessary to control the way the child's body uses calcium.

Plenty of fruits and vegetables, with daily meat or fish, or *dal* and lentils, will ensure an adequate supply of other minerals and vitamins. Whenever possible, the foods should be fresh or, failing that, frozen rather than dried or canned. For instance, frozen peas contain nearly as much vitamin C as fresh peas do, but dried or tinned processed peas contain no vitamin C at all fruit juices will supplement a child's vitamin C intake. But there is no point in trying to force a child to eat a particular food.

Between 6 months and 1 year, breast milk alone is not sufficient to provide all nutrients needed to maintain growth. Supplementary foods have to be introduced.

An ideal time is very necessary to introduce supplementary foods. If you introduce them too early, chances of undermining future eating habits cannot be ruled out. Waiting too long can also lead to some difficulties when an infant may resist foods, may not want to chew, etc.

While introducing supplements, do them one at a time. Small portions, starting with a teaspoon, would be better. Always start the foods with a thin consistency, gradually thickening them. If a child does not like a particular food item, do not force him to eat it. You can try feeding it at a later stage. Limited salt should be used, and strain the food to get a smooth consistency.

When the infant is able to chew, you can introduce finely chopped soft fruits instead of pureed foods. This will probably be when they cut their first four teeth.

You can start with quarter teaspoon of egg yolk that is a rich source of vitamin A, B-complex and iron. If he has loose stools, or he throws up, then you can introduce it later. Ripe mashed banana in a teaspoon can be given at first. Or you may give stewed apple, cooked and pureed pears or peaches, pureed and strained orange.

Cooked and strained carrots, beans, peas, spinach, tomatoes can be introduced from six months onwards. Chicken or meat in the form of soups can be introduced around the eighth month.

It is wrong to overfeed a child. Overweight babies are susceptible to illness, particularly chest infections, and they are likely to grow into overweight children and then into obese adults.

Nearly every child will overeat if given the chance, and once a baby has become used to eating too much, it is difficult to break the habit.

Many babies eat cereals and processed baby foods in the first few months of life. But the mother must remember that as the amount of this food is increased, the amount of milk should be reduced. The total fluid requirement should be made up with water flavoured with fruit juice. The total volume of liquid depends on the weight of the baby – about 25 fluid ounces for a four and a half kilo baby.

By the age of nine months, many babies have settled into a routine of three meals a day, mostly of processed baby foods. But there are others who have started to eat the same food as the rest of the family – small helpings of meat, vegetables and potatoes – and grow perfectly normal.

Like adults, babies too need minerals and vitamins. Calcium, iron and other minerals are essential for growth. Vitamins are best supplied from fresh foods – particularly fruit and vegetables, eggs and fish.

A child who is reared only on tinned baby foods is unlikely to be under-nourished, because many of these have vitamins added to them. During the first year of a baby's life it is wise to add some fruit juice, like orange, containing vitamin C, to the diet. After the first year, a child on a normal mixed diet should need no vitamin supplements.

7
NUTRITION FOR TODDLERS

Your child's nutritional needs increase with his growth proportionately. He needs larger quantities as he learns to walk. As he steps into his second and third years of age, the same diet may be continued, but in increased quantities.

His diet should include sufficient amounts of protein, carbohydrates, fats, vitamins and minerals. These he will get so long as he has a variety of foods. As he is still growing he still needs more protein and calories for his body weight than an adult.

Though, generally speaking, a variety of carbohydrates, fruits and vegetables, and protein-rich foods will be ample for your child's needs, some foods have particular nutritional value. All fruits and vegetables provide carbohydrates and fibre, but for minerals you need leafy vegetables, and citrus fruits as a good source of vitamins A and C . For a balanced diet for your toddler, choose foods from each of the groups in the chart.

Nutrients Provided by Different Foods

Food Groups	*Nutrients*
Breads & Cereals	
Wholemeal bread, noodles, rice, pasta, chapati	Protein, carbohydrates, iron, B vitamins, calcium
Citrus Fruits	
Oranges, lemons, limes, grapes	Vitamins A and C
Fats	
Butter, ghee, oil, fish oils, margarine	Vitamins A and D, essential fatty acids
Green & Yellow Vegetables	
Cabbage, spinach, beans, lettuce, celery, yellow pumpkin	Minerals including calcium, chlorine, chromium, cobalt, copper, fluorine, manganese, magnesium, potassium, sodium, zinc
High Protein Foods	
Chicken, fish, beef, eggs, cheese, nuts, legumes, dal	Protein, fat, iron, vitamins A and D, B vitamins, especially B12
Milk & Dairy Products	
Milk, cream, curds, ice-cream, cheese	Protein, fat, calcium, vitamins A and D, B vitamins
Other Vegetables & Fruits	
Potatoes, beetroot, carrots, cauliflower, apples, apricots, pineapple, bananas, strawberries	Carbohydrates, vitamins A, B and C

Plan snacks also for the whole day's nutrition, and coordinate meals and snacks so that you serve different foods for each meal.

Milk and milk-based drinks are good at snack-time, as they contain protein, calcium and many of the B vitamins. Try using only whole milk until your child is three years old. After this you can use semi-skimmed milk, but not skimmed milk, unless your child is overweight. You can also give fresh fruit juice, for it is rich in vitamin C.

Your child may be bored eating the same type of food every day. So provide variety. You can cut the bread slices with a cutter into interesting shapes and using lots of jam or small bits of fruit placed on the cut bread, making them appealing to the kid.

You can include wheat porridge (or oats), made of broken wheat (*dalia*), powder groundnuts, a little jaggery and milk. This makes for a wholesome food.

You can make sweet *rotis* by adding 1 tbsp of soya powder to 1 cup wheat flour and 1 tbsp jaggery. These rotis can be made small and used as snacks.

If you are giving him idlis or plain chapatis, you can enhance their nutritive value by adding carrots and peas to the idlis, and spinach, mint on fenugreek (methi) leaves to the chapatis.

Your toddler may reject a food in one form, but given in another form may eat it with gusto. For example, curd can be sweetened and chilled and served as ice-cream.

A child normally likes to snack more often than an adult, as his meals are smaller and he cannot eat large meals. Snacking is just as healthy as meals, and it keeps their energy going instead of making them hungry, tired and irritable. Never bribe them to eat what they do not like. Some children do not like to drink milk often. You can give other milk products instead. Since the appetite of the child changes from day to day, do not be upset if he misses out on milk or some other food for a day. Be sure that your child's appetite is good, else consult a paediatrician.

8
NUTRITION FOR OLDER CHILDREN

The normal child has a steady growth in terms of height and weight, once he starts going to school. His food habits gradually undergo a change in the beginning of the school years. You may find that he does not like to eat his breakfast, or has no interest in eating his lunch, or has no appetite for any food. These may be due to changes in the environment and his interest that is now diverted to playtime. This is probably the time when parents have to be careful to see that their child is not getting exposed to junk foods at this age. Just like the pre-school kid, the school-going child's nutrition requirements remain the same, except that the quantity increases.

Your child now needs more proteins. So include more protein foods like egg, nuts and lentils in your child's diet. More calcium is needed for the growth of bones, hence, see that he gets substantial quantities of milk and milk products, curds, cheese and paneer. He also needs foods that are rich in vitamin C, and more calories, so have him eat more complex carbohydrates like wheat bread, chapati, potatoes, etc.

Most medical people think that breakfast is the most important meal of the day. But pressures of early morning make them either skip it or have a very light one.

It is important that your child wakes up early, and has enough time to eat a good breakfast before going to school. Give him something that he likes, rather than force him to eat something he has no liking for. At the same time, be sure that what he eats is nutritious. Plan his breakfast in such a way that the simple and nutritious breakfast that he eats makes him enjoy it.

Recommended Calories

Age	*Approximate body Weight (kgs)*	*Approximate Kcals/kg*
Babies	5.4 – 8.6	108
Toddlers	12.2	1240
4-6 years	19	1690
7-9 years	26.9	1950
10-12 years (boys)	35.4	2190
10-12 years (girls)	31.5	1970

Source: Recommended Dietary Allowances for India, ICMR, 1996.

Average Height of Boys at Various Ages

Age	*Weight (kgs)*	*Height (cm)*
Birth	3.3	50.5
3 months	6.0	61.1
6 months	7.8	67.8
9 months	9.2	72.3

Contd...

1 year	10.2	76.1
2 years	12.3	85.6
3 years	14.6	94.9
4 years	16.7	102.9
5 years	18.7	109.9
6 years	20.7	116.1
7 years	22.9	121.7
8 years	25.3	127.0
9 years	28.1	132.2
10 years	31.4	137.5
11 years	32.2	140.0
12 years	37.0	147.0

Source: Nutrient Requirement and Recommended Dietary Allowances for Indians, ICMR, 1990.

Average Height and Weight of Girls at Various Ages

Age	*Weight (kgs)*	*Height (cm)*
Birth	3.2	49.9
3 months	5.4	60.2
6 months	7.2	66.6
9 months	8.6	71.1
1 year	9.5	75.0
2 years	11.8	84.5
3 years	14.1	93.9
4 years	16.0	101.6

Contd...

5 years	17.7	108.4
6 years	19.5	114.6
7 years	21.8	120.6
8 years	24.8	126.4
9 years	28.5	132.2
10 years	32.5	138.3
11 years	33.7	142.0
12 years	38.7	148.0

Source: Nutrient Requirement and Recommended Dietary Allowances for Indians, ICMR, 1990.

9

BATHING AND HYGIENE

Besides rest, diet and exercise, every child needs to follow a regimen of hygiene and cleanliness. A newborn baby's skin is soft and delicate, so you must handle the baby with care. Generally, there is a popular belief that even babies need a bath every day. Not so is the case. With all the diaper changes and wiping of mouth and nose feedings, most babies need to be bathed every day. But even with this you need to maintain hygiene, especially take care of their bottom.

The nappy is an absolute essential item of a baby's equipments. But the nappy can also lead to nappy rash. Since the nappy is always in contact with the baby's very soft skin, it creates a warm and moist environment, which promotes growth of bacteria. Compounded with this is the constant friction causing chafing. This results in an uncomfortable and painful problem for the baby.

To ensure that there are no nappy rashes, change nappies frequently. Use nappies made of very soft cotton. Gently clean the baby's bottom with comfortably warm water, and dry thoroughly between the folds every time the nappy is changed. Always wipe from front to back, so that faecal matter does not get into the genital area to cause infection.

Baby oil will be useful in removing any dried material on the skin. If there is nappy rash, apply a barrier cream containing zinc oxide to protect the skin. Rinsing the nappies thoroughly after washing them is absolutely essential so that any detergent that may still be present in the washed nappies does not affect the baby's skin.

Baths for the babies can be given at a time convenient to the mother. While some like to bathe them around noon, there are some who like to give them at night before putting them to sleep. Any time convenient is good enough, but make sure the baby is not very hungry.

Bath time with the baby is a special time for close bondage between mother and baby. A warm bath can soothe a restless baby and help him sleep letter. Initially, sponge baths would do until the umbilical cord falls off.

If you use a shampoo to wash the baby's head, use a washcloth that is dipped in warm water, add a few drops of shampoo, and gently apply on the scalp. Holding the baby firmly with your arm under his back, and your wrist and hand supporting his neck, you can use a faucet or a mug of water to rinse the hair.

After thoroughly drying the hair, use a soft baby brush to comb the baby's hair. As far as possible, avoid using a hair dryer to dry your baby's hair.

Moisturise your baby's skin with a mild moisturising lotion. Dust talc on to your palms, and smooth it gently on his skin. Check the navel area for redness, moisture or swelling. Keep it dry and clean at all times even after the cord has fallen off.

Most toddlers like to have a bath as they consider it playtime. This would be an ideal time for you to teach him how to wash himself. You can give him a pretty, colourful sponge, and let him handle it himself. You can teach him how to use the sponge on his face, then his arms and legs, and so on. Since he is too young to do a fine job of washing himself thoroughly, you need to do the washing all over again after he has done it initially. Soap his hands and show him how to spread the soap over the body and arms; then make a game of rinsing off the soap.

It is always better to give the toddler a bath when he has had his breakfast, so that he can enjoy his bath and play. The earlier you teach hygiene to your child, the better, and the best way of teaching is by example. Wash your hands in the presence of your child, show him how you soap your hands and rinse them. Then both of you can soap each other's hands, and then wash each other's hands. Then inspect each other's hands to see whose is the cleanest.

It is essential for your child to know that every time he uses the lavatory, he needs to wash his hands. Also that he has to wash his hands well before and after his meals. Teach him how to rinse his hands under a tap, making sure he knows which is the hot tap and which is the cold. Most toddlers are keen to do thing for themselves – washing their own face, for example – so there is the risk that your child may turn on the hot tap, or grab the soap or shampoo and get it in his eyes.

Check the temperature of the water before your child gets into the bath water. Check that the taps are closed tightly.

If you keep pets at home, you may be concerned about the possible health risks to your toddler. Never allow your child to kiss the pet, especially near its nose and mouth. Encourage him to always wash his hands after playing with the pet, and especially before he eats anything.

By the time your toddler is three years old, he will be more interested in playing rather than spending his time in bathing and washing. The best way to get him into a bathing routine is to turn the task of bathing into a game filled with fun. You can allow him each day the soap that he would like to use, or a particular shampoo, or towel, or which toy he would like to bathe that day as he is washing himself. Do not rush him with his task, as this might not give him satisfaction, and the next time he might be reluctant to have a bath. Do not leave bath time till sleep time, for he may not then enjoy it. When he washes his hair, make it fun for him by letting him peep into the mirror to see what he looks like with all the suds in his hair.

Let your child have his own towel, soap dish, shampoo, mug, etc. You can also provide his own laundry basket so that he can discard his dirty clothes in it. Encourage him to change his underwear and socks daily.

Hair Care

By the time your child is 18 months old, he should be having a thick crop of hair. It will need regular washing to remove everyday grime. Most toddlers do not like hair washing, so keep the hair short. This will make it easier to brush also. See that the shampoo that he uses is very mild.

School-going children most often pick up lice from other children who do not take care of their hair. There are special shampoos available to treat nits. Cleanliness is the main consideration, and regular washing of the hair will keep lice and nits away.

With your child mingling with other children in the neighbourhood and in school, he can be affected by ringworm also. This is a contagious disease, and can be spread by direct contact. It causes an itchy skin eruption that spreads out from the side of the infection on the scalp, and sometimes nails. These scaly patches on the scalp are usually oval in shape. While the edges of the patch remain scaly, the centre clears, leaving rings. Scratching must be avoided to prevent spreading the ringworm from one part of the body to another and to prevent secondary bacterial infections. Consult your doctor for treatment.

10
BOWEL AND BLADDER TRAINING

Training a baby to control his or her bowels and bladder is a needless cause of worry to many parents. Sooner or later, all children become clean and dry–five-year-olds do not normally need to wear nappies.

There is no point in starting to train a baby until he or she can sit up easily. By nine months, the baby will probably have settled into a pattern of passing a motion once or twice a day. Often this happens at regular times, such as shortly after his mid-day meal.

Sit the baby on the pot for five minutes or so at that time. If he passes a motion, praise him; if not, put him in a nappy and wait for the next time. Soon he associates the feel of the pot on his bottom with the feeling of passing a motion, and increasingly often the first sensation becomes the stimulus for the second.

But the control of the bowels becomes well established before starting to train the baby to control his bladder. Again the principle is to sit the child on the pot in the hope that he will by chance pass water. Give praise for success but do not make an issue about a dry pot.

By the age of 15 months or so a baby should be able to learn simple words for passing urine and bowel motions. When teaching him these words remember that he or you will need to use them in front of other people for some years, so short, inoffensive terms should be used.

Most children grasp the idea of pot training quickly enough. It is then infuriating when they lapse, soiling a nappy within a minute or so of a fruitless 10-minute squat on the pot. Never scold a baby for this. Sometimes this happens when a child is under stress – perhaps he is just learning to walk, or another baby is born in the family and he is jealous, or his father has been away from home. Patience and perseverance are the best ways of dealing with this situation.

Some children love to play with their faeces or urine. The mother should make an effort to suppress any disgust she may feel, since this may cause the child to feel distressed about 'dirtying' his clean pot, and set him back in his pot training.

Girls are generally more receptive than boys to being taught good habits of toilet hygiene; girls are generally neater than boys and will enjoy turning a cleanliness routine into a game. Boys are often messier than girls in using the potty or the toilet.

The first sign that your child's bladder control is developing is when he becomes aware of the passage of urine, and he may try to attract your attention and point to his nappy. As he grows older and able to control his urine, you may find that his nappy is dry after a nap. You can encourage him to empty his bladder before going to bed and as soon as he wakes up.

A child of two or three cannot hold on to urine for much more than four to five hours. So control of the bladder during the night is the last to come. Once he gets used to controlling his bladder and remaining dry throughout the night, you can do away with nappies for his. But be sure to have a rubber sheet on the mattress and below a cotton sheet to protect the mattress.

A three-year-old child has fairly reliable bladder and bowel control, but occasional accidents do occur. They may happen when your child's bladder is full and he refuses to use the lavatory in a strange place, or he is so engrossed in his game that he ignores it. You must point out to them the necessity of emptying out their bladder at regular intervals.

There are some children with late development of brain-bladder link, and hence the control of their bladder and bowel may take longer. Most of the time this is a hereditary factor.

Bed-wetting

A child who wets his bed does feel embarrassed, especially if he is over the age of four or five. Try to reassure him that it was accident and that he will not wet again. In a child who has been reliably dry for some time, regression to night or daytime wetting is usually a sign of anxiety. It can also be caused by an infection of the urinary tract.

It is quite common for children up to the age of five to bed-wet at night. Boys are more prone to it than girls. Most grow out of this habit in a natural way; if you do go out, remember to carry a spare set of clothes. Be sympathetic and make light of any accidents.

Constipation

Some children have constipation without any other illness signs. It is nothing to worry about unless your child feels discomfort. Then consult your doctor. Do not administer any laxatives to your child.

A varied diet with plenty of fresh fruits and vegetables with complex carbohydrates will ease the problem. Green leafy vegetables and oatmeal contain cellulose, which holds water in the stools, making them bulky and soft so that the child has an easy bowel evacuation. Dried figs and stewed prunes also help during constipation.

If the stools are hard, the child may be reluctant to empty his bowels, and he holds on to them to prevent the pain while evacuating his bowel. He may also not use strange toilets; even in school he may be reluctant to relieve himself.

Sometimes a few days of constipation may follow after an illness with high temperature. This may be because your child has had very little to eat, and has lost water in the form of sweating. He will soon get back to normal, so don't worry.

11

SLEEP AND WAKEFULNESS

Everybody needs to sleep and relax. The amount of sleep varies with age, and from person to person. A newborn baby sleeps most of the time, and wakes up only when hungry or uncomfortable due to wetting the nappy. Each infant evolves for itself various internal clocks that help to establish regular patterns of hunger, sleep and wakefulness.

As the baby grows he has to be helped to sleep by gentle rocking or soft music. Some babies cry themselves to sleep. Some like to suck their thumbs, some go to sleep while being fed.

A child aged one to two years needs 14-15 hours of sleep, three to four-year-old needs around 12 hours of sleep, while those between four and six years need about 11 hours of sleep. Older children need roughly about eight to ten hours of sleep.

To ensure that your child has adequate rest, be sure that his bed is comfortable, and there is minimum noise in his room. Do not cover him in too many clothes, which may make him uncomfortable. Tell him pleasant stories while putting him to sleep so that he has no fears at night. See that the atmosphere in the house is healthy and pleasant, with a lot of love and understanding amongst the family members. Be sure that your child has been well fed, that he has emptied his bladder before hopping into bed.

Many children wake up periodically during the night. If your child too wakes up regularly, never hesitate to go him and comfort him. Some fear deep down in him may be the cause for his waking up often, and he may not be able to pinpoint the reason. He needs a lot of assurance and comfort to tide over this phase, and patience pays, though it may be harassing for you, especially if you are a working mother.

The time for going to bed should be consistent, but this should not be rigid. If a child is playing and enjoying himself immensely allow him this pleasure for another 15-20 minutes.

Daytime Nap

As your child grows older, he may not want to sleep at naptime, but it would be wiser to coax him to sleep for he does need rest. He may also get 'cranky' due to tiredness and may not be able to express himself. You can read out to him or play some soft music that may put him to sleep. Even if he sleeps for just half an hour, he will feel refreshed and ready to face the day with renewed energy.

Transition from Cot to Bed

As your infant grows up and is strong enough to climb out of his cot and come into your room, consider it a time of transition from cot to bed. This would excite most children, but initially find the bed a strange place to sleep in, and hence have a restless night. Place all his familiar and favourite toys in his new bed, and consider keeping a dim night-light on in the room. If he still seems restless, you can let him have his naps in the morning in it till he becomes familiar with it. Once he is settled in, sit with him for some time, read or tell a story till he falls asleep before leaving him. Once he gets used to this routine, even if he does not fall asleep, you can wish him goodnight and leave him, though do not close his door.

After the age of three, children usually find some delaying tactics to put off going to bed. How you handle this depends on individuals. You may not mind sitting with him for a long time, telling him story after story, but if you are a working mother, your patience may wear out thin. But never show your impatience, for all children need the assurance of your presence in the room.

To be sure that your child has a restful night, be sure that he goes to sleep in a happy frame of mind. Bed times should be happy times, and though you may admonish him during daytime for any misdemeanour, you would not like him to go to sleep with the sound of an angry parent's voice echoing in his ears.

If you have more than one child, sharing a room would help your younger child to have a sound sleep. Company is so very reassuring.

Fear of the Dark

As your child grows older, his imagination too starts becoming fertile. He is capable of imaging something horrifying or frightening in the shadows. It is very normal for a child, and even an adult, to have a fear of darkness, or the unknown. So leave a night-light on in the room or in the corridor outside with the door open. You can even have it in the bathroom if it is attached to the room, so that with the door open light can filter in into the bedroom. If you use a night-light, be sure that it does not cast shadows. Never ridicule the child for being frightened. Assure him that you are close by, and if he is frightened when he wakes up, he can come to you for a cuddle.

Privacy

You must encourage your child to have respect for privacy. He can have his own private space, which will be his alone. He can keep all his belongings and favourite things there. Most children respond quickly to the idea of privacy, especially if they are given their own room where they can proudly display all that they treasure. You can teach him how to keep this private area of his neat, and encourage him to put away all his toys neatly after he has played with them. This will inculcate in him the habit of maintaining cleanliness.

You can teach your child to stay within his own space as early as two years, but definitely by three when he is receptive to reason. He will learn that just like you respect his privacy, he too needs to respect your privacy. But never try to shut him out of your room, but gently teach him how he should respect your privacy. It may take time as he has never before been alone, and he may need a lot of assurances and comfort before he becomes comfortable with the new set-up. You need to spend more time with him while he is in bed awake, but eventually he will settle down.

12

TEETH AND EYE CARE

The teeth begin to form in the embryo, months before a baby is born; they develop from a core of cells in the centre of each jaw. This core gradually grows backwards on each side, through the areas, which eventually become hardened as jawbones.

Small side branches of cells break off and form tooth buds, one bud for each tooth, making 52 buds in all. These develop into tooth shapes, and then start to form the hard dental tissues—enamel, dentine and cement—to become fully formed teeth, embedded in the gums.

At birth, all the deciduous teeth are formed, except for their roots. The tips of the first permanent teeth are formed, except for their roots. The tips of the first permanent molars are also hardened, although these teeth do not emerge until the child is about six or eight years old.

Babies cut their first milk teeth at about six to eight months; and the last ones, the second molars, are through by about two-and-a-half to three years. These times vary widely, however, from child to child, and a few babies are born with teeth already showing. At seven to eight months, two upper teeth appear, and at nine to ten months, four-more teeth, and so on, until there are no milk teeth.

The first permanent molars grow into place behind the milk teeth at about six years old. Then the milk teeth come away, pushed out by the growth of their permanent successors. This is usually a painless process, the milk tooth being shed with virtually no bleeding if allowed enough time.

The deciduous incisors are replaced at seven to eight years of age, and the deciduous molars are gone by the age of 10-13. The second permanent molars emerge at about 15, and the third molars, or wisdom teeth, at 15-25, although often they are impacted (jammed by neighbouring teeth) and may never grow fully.

Teething is usually a painless process. If a baby does have trouble teething, it is usually between the ages of 12 and 18 months when the first four molar teeth are appearing. The baby may lose his appetite, and wake and cry during the night. A bottle of warm milk will probably pacify him, but the baby should not be removed from his cot; and the practice should stop when teeth are through, otherwise he will expect middle-of-the-night feeding.

Most babies want to put things into their mouths and gnaw when teething. There is no harm in this. You can provide a hard rubber teething ring that the baby can hold easily.

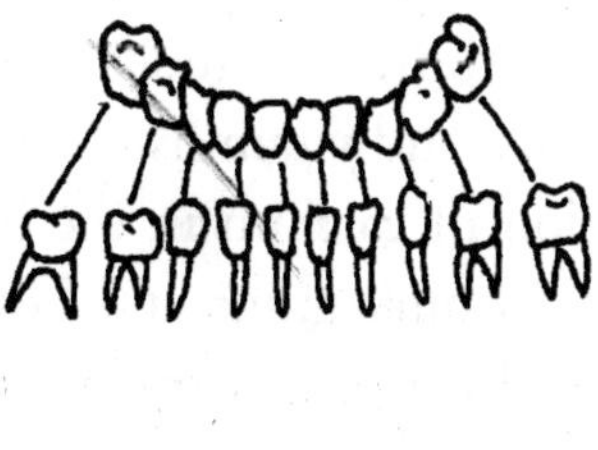

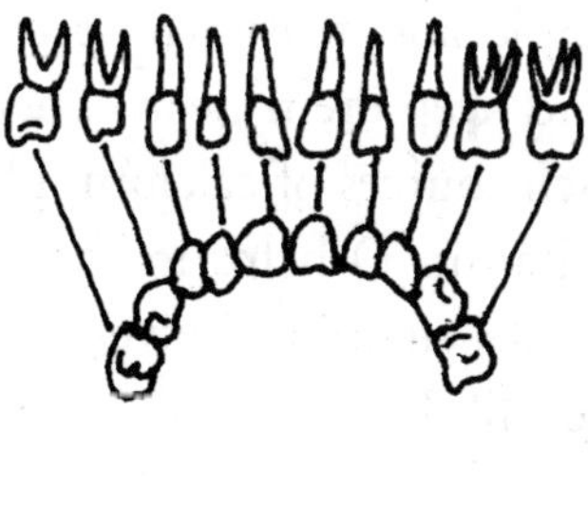

You have been brushing your child's teeth from the time that they first appeared. You should continue to do so at least twice a day. A child should clean his teeth, by brushing up and down with a pure bristle brush. The brush has to be soft and small, and use toothpaste, which has fluoride. Always brush your child's teeth after the meal at night so that there is no food particles left in the mouth overnight. He should also brush them before going to bed.

As your toddler grows older, he would like to hold the brush and brush his teeth by himself. This should be encouraged, but since he would not be able to clean them effectively, you should finish with a thorough brushing.

Sweet foods and biscuits should not be eaten between meals. The worst feature of child health, especially in Western countries, is the amount of dental decay. This is chiefly caused by a diet too rich in sugar and carbohydrates. But most decay can be prevented if children are taught to care for their teeth.

Regular visits, at least twice a year, to a dentist for a check-up should begin at about three or four years of age. If baby teeth are lost before the age of six, the growing permanent teeth lack the support they need. Fluoridation of public water suppliers in some areas prevents tooth decay, but its benefits are wasted if the child's diet is wrong.

Up to the age of two years, infants should be given fresh apple and toast whose coarseness helps to scour the teeth and keep them clean. Then you can introduce foods that are rich sources of calcium, phosphorus, and vitamins C and D. Vitamin D helps in the absorption of calcium in the body, while vitamin C gives the child its pink gums and healthy teeth. Fluorine also enhances the promotion of teeth formation, and prevents tooth decay. Hence fluoride toothpaste is a must for your child.

Eye Care

Vitamins A and B are essential for children to have sparkling and clear eyes. Vitamin A prevents night blindness, eye strain and fatigue. It also helps the tear ducts in secreting moisture, which gives eyes their sparkle. Babies can be given vitamin A drops orally, which can be fed in a spoon or by a dropper into the mouth, in the first month of their birth.

As your infant grows into a toddler, when he shows interest in seeing the pictures in a book, be sure that the room is well lit. Natural light is best during daytime, so ensure that your child's room gets plenty of sunshine and air. At night, be sure that enough light falls on the book, which he is seeing or reading.

Make sure that your child is not put to any eye strain. See that he does not read in very dazzling or dim light. Initially, check that the books the child reads has large prints. If he watches television, be sure to have a soft indirect lighting in the room, and let your child watch it from a distance of at least eight feet.

If you suspect your child of having difficulty in focusing or having a blurred vision, see an eye specialist immediately. If he advises wearing spectacles for improvement of sight, see that he gets a pair as early as possible, and that he wears them at once. He should remove them from time to time, and close his eyes for at least five minutes, then blink a dozen times before wearing them again. This helps to relax his eye muscles.

A child may suddenly develop squint between the ages of two and six years. This can be cured if it is attended to immediately. It is common for a baby to have crossed eyes in the first couple of months, but by the third month they become steady and straight.

Some babies have watery eyes but they clear up by the time they turn one year. You may also notice a discharge from the corner of the eyes. White matter collects in the corner of the eye and along the edges of the lids. This discharge will make the lids stick together, caused by obstructed tear ducts. But even this is a passing phase. Wet a small ball of cotton and gently wipe the matter away. Do not apply pressure at all.

If some grit or foreign particle gets into your child's eye, you can remove it by drawing the upper eyelid down and away from the eye, and holding it by the lashes. This allows the tears to wash the grit out of the eye. Otherwise you can ask your child to open the eye into a cup of water and blink a couple of times. If this too proves unsuccessful, take him to see a doctor, but see that he does not rub his eye. He can hold a soft cloth or a wad of cotton on his affected eye till the doctor sees him.

13

DENTAL DEVELOPMENT

A common source of parental concern is regarding the teething of their child. They are worried when the child will cut his first tooth. As is true with all types of development, there is no fixed or ideal time when the first tooth should erupt. In some children, it may erupt as early as 5 months, while in others, it may not erupt upto the age of 1 year. There is nothing wrong with your child if his tooth doesn't come out by 1 year. Most of the parents think that their child is deficient in calcium and/or vitamin-D, which may be true, but only in a few cases. In majority of cases, it is just a normal variant and hence no intervention is required.

Parents also attribute a lot of things to teething. Every complaint at the time of teething is attributed to it. Thus if the child has fever, irritability, diarrhoea etc, the parents usually blame it on the teething process. While the child may be a bit irritable during the period due to discomfort, things like fever, vomiting etc. cannot be attributed to teething. It is true that during the teething phase, there is irritation on the gums of the child and to reduce it, he puts foreign objects in his mouth and chews on them. These foreign objects may be an indirect source of infection in the child and cause diarrhoea.

There are two types of teeth: deciduous or the milk teeth and the permanent teeth. There are 20 milk teeth and 32 permanent teeth. The milk teeth start erupting from the age of 5 months onwards and the first tooth to come is usually the lower central incisor.

A simple way to remember the eruption of milk teeth is that by 6 months there are 0 teeth; by 12 months, 6 teeth; by 18 months, 12 teeth; and by 24 months, 16 teeth. The last 4 teeth make their appearance by 2½-3 years.

The permanent teeth start erupting 2½ from the age of 6-7 years onwards. A little before that the milk teeth are shed. This process continues on and by the age of 12-13 years, the child has 28 teeth. The last 4 teeeth, popularly known as the wisdom teeth, erupt at a variable age, in the late teens or early twenties.

Chronology of Eruption of Milk Teeth and the Permanent Teeth

Milk Teeth

Teeth	Age
1 lower central incisors	5-10 months
2 upper central incisors	8-12 months
2 upper lateral incisors	9-13 months
2 lower lateral incisors	13-16 months
2 upper anterior molars	13-17 months
4 canines	12-22 months
4 posterior molars	24-30 months

Permanent Teeth

Teeth	Age
First molars	6-7 years
Incisors	7-9 years
Premolars	9-11 years
Canines	10-12 years
Second molars	12-16 years
Third molars	17-25 years

14
SKIN CARE

An important function of the skin is to act as a barrier against invasion by germs. Heredity gives one the colour of one's skin, and one needs to take special care of it right from babyhood.

If your baby is born with dark fuzzy hair on his face, arms and legs, make a paste of gram flour (*besan*) with milk-cream and rose water, and apply this paste on his face and limbs for a few minutes. Then give him his regular bath. Make sure that the paste does not dry on the baby's skin. If it does, then wet the area and allow the caked area to soften before washing it.

Functions of the Skin

As stated earlier, the skin is the body's greatest barrier against invasion of germs. It is the body's largest organ, and guards the organs inside the body. It regulates the body's temperature. The highly sensitive nerve endings on the skin put a baby in touch with the outside world. In fact, it is through the skin that they experience the tender and loving touch of their parents.

Special Baby Skin Care

A baby's skin is very tender and needs a lot of care. The outer layer (dermis) is not completely developed with its elastic fibres. So that fragile skin is susceptible to damage and is very sensitive to touch.

The baby's skin is quite a thin layer. It can absorb anything that is applied on its surface. So you must be careful that his skin is free of any harmful or strong lotions. A baby cream application, especially in winter, will be absorbed easily and keep the skin supple and elastic.

Since the production of melanin (a protective pigment) is low in babies, exposure to the sun should be avoided, except probably a few minutes to absorb vitamin D from the sun's rays. Too much exposure to the sun will easily burn the skin and lead to chafing.

Babies need special care of their skin with frequent change of nappies, continuous wiping and cleaning of the nappy area, and around the mouth and nose. If these are not handled carefully chances of infection and skin damage are high.

Avoid using irritants like harsh soaps and detergents. Always use a mild, gentle soap and shampoo for the baby's bath. Baby creams and lotions are available, and are safe to use.

When your baby passes stools, be sure that you clean the area well with warm water and a gentle cleaning product. Then pat the area dry with a very soft cloth, and dust baby power on that area. This helps to reduce friction between the skin and the clothing, and guards against penetration of irritating or foreign substances through the skin.

Keep your baby's skin normally dry, not moist. Apply talcum powder whenever you feel the skin is moist, especially around the nappy area. You can avoid excessive moisture less from the baby's skin by using baby cream and lotion.

Dress the infant in loose-fitting clothes. On warm nights cover the baby with a thin sheet instead of using a flannel or thin blanket. See that the nappies and clothes that he wears are made of fine cotton that is soft to the touch. Loose clothes allow air circulation, and keep the baby dry and comfortable, away from the clammy heat of summer.

Once the baby grows older, it is easier to manage the care of his skin. he still needs creams in winter, but his resilience is stronger than other babies.

A lot depends on the diet that is followed. Too many sweet and fatty foods will only lead to indigestion and freckles. If your child is fond of sweets, give him ones made at home. You can substitute honey for sugar, for not only is honey nutritious, it is also good for the skin. Introduce your child to fresh fruit juice instead of bottled or aerated drinks.

15

TOYS AND GAMES

Play is both serious and important to a child – it is the way he learns about the world. Even a baby needs something to focus on once he is able to control his eye movements. A baby may be interested in a rattle, the tinkling of small bells, squeaky rubber animals or cuddly animals. These toys can amuse infants up to the age of one, for this is the time they can listen, look, handle and chew.

Children in the age group of 1-2 years like toys that make a noise, and something that they can pull or push, bang and make noise. They love to take apart or dismantle a particular toy, and try to re-assemble it.

The older toddlers like to play with toys that exercise their imagination. These include building blocks, dolls, cars, crayons, balls, etc. A small boy pulling an empty shoebox along the floor by a piece of string is not, in his mind, playing. He is in charge of a bus–and is learning that the bus must go round obstacles and not through them. He finds that the box runs more easily on a tiled floor than on a carpet, that the harder he pulls, the faster the box moves, and that, unless he keeps the box level, it overturns. These are all learning skills.

Simple toys are more versatile, so they have durability and are better for imaginative play. Toys with various colours, textures, shapes and noises will stimulate all five senses.

Infants enjoy games that involve building, 'putting in and taking out' games, so bricks of plastic of different sizes are ideal. As he grows older, his skills too develop, and he will be able to play with interlocking blocks and more advanced shape-sorters.

Pre-school children enjoy dabbling in drawing, painting and imaginative play. Give your child painting and drawing materials to allow him to develop his mental creativity.

Your role as teacher starts as soon as your baby is born. The time you spend with him helps him in becoming aware of his surroundings, in the development of coordination of hand and eye movements, and various other skills. Your child's development will centre on play and this is the most natural way for him to learn. Toys therefore have a significant educational role in all your child's developmental milestones.

Your toddler's mobility and independence will be enhanced by sturdy, wheeled walking toys. A pushbike can be used indoor as well as out, and will improve your child's muscle strength and coordination.

When you are travelling you will need toys to distract your child. Magnetised games are particularly useful in cars because the bits and pieces cannot get lost. You can stick velcro on certain toys so that they stick to the car seat and stay in one place while your child is playing with them.

When your child begins to play and walk, pay attention to the way he uses his toys. Make his playthings appealing by arranging them in an imaginative order. Do not keep buying toys for him regularly. Instead, encourage him to interact with the existing toys in different ways – like the boy with the shoebox who used it as a bus.

A child does not need elaborate toys; sand, water, clay, pebbles and wooden blocks give him the chance for the kind of play that develops experience and muscular coordination. Playing develops the physical, emotional and intellectual faculties of a child.

16
STAGES OF CHILD DEVELOPMENT

During the pre-school years, every child learns to master dozens of skills as his body and brain develop sufficiently for him to be able to tackle them. A baby who is given a lot of attention – who is loved, handled, played with and talked to – generally achieves his milestones of physical development earlier than one left in the cot all day.

In addition, a child who is secure in a stable family, and who mixes with other children of the same age, develops quickly both socially and intellectually. A young child needs real-life experience: he needs to touch, taste and handle different things.

Stages in Baby's Growth

At birth, the baby is able to suckle and has a powerful grip, but uses only the fingers. He may respond to a sudden loud noise, but not to ordinary sounds. He can see, although objects are blurred. Crying is the only means of expressing discomfort or hunger.

A baby 3-4 months old turns his head towards sounds. When he is placed face downwards, he can lift his chin off the mattress. He still sleeps most of the day.

A 7-8-month-old baby can hold his head firmly erect and sit without support. By now he has learnt to use thumbs to grip. Eyes now move in unison; he hears everything and reacts immediately. He puts objects in his mouth. Two upper teeth appear.

A 11-12-month-old infant stands with slight support. He walks holding on to furniture. He can speak single words, and push light objects about, close and open doors, and crawl rapidly. His first molar teeth appear.

At 13-14 months, the infant walks without support. He feeds himself with a spoon. Being very sound conscious he can locate the source of the sound. He can understand much of the simple language, and starts to use one or two words correctly.

At 18 months, the child walks up and down stairs, one hand holding the rail. He can drink from a cup without spilling much milk. He asks for the pot when he wants to empty his bowel. He can use words of up to 20 intelligible words, but understands four or five times that number. By now he has 12-16 teeth.

A two-year-old child dresses himself but cannot yet fasten buttons. He has started to put words together into short phrases, and to ask questions. He is by now usually dry at night. He may begin to play with other children.

How Babies Grow

A young mother often worries unnecessarily about her baby's growth. As the boy next door can walk and talk at 12 months, and her baby can do neither at the same age, it does not mean that there is anything wrong. It is likely that at 18 months her baby will have caught up with, and possibly overtaken, the neighbours baby in both mental and physical development. Even if a child seems to be mentally and physically advanced for his age, it does not necessarily mean that he will be a bright child at school.

With rare exceptions, all babies eventually walk, talk, control their bladders, and learn to feed themselves. If a baby is late in achieving a particular ability, it is rarely a matter of concern. But if all normal developments are delayed, then a doctor should be consulted.

Starting to Walk

Walking is one of the most variable milestones of childhood. Children may walk as early as 10 months, or as late as 18 months. A baby of only six or seven months will attempt to make stepping movement if supported by the armpits. Well before his first birthday, he finds some way of getting about–usually by crawling, shuffling along on his bottom, or paddling along sideways like a crab.

Some children spend only a short time at this stage of development, and walk soon afterwards. Others, who may have found an efficient way of crawling, show no inclination to begin walking. None of this matters if the child's muscular development and control are normal – for example, if the child is using his hands to examine things and is beginning to feed himself.

How a Baby Learns to Talk

Children have some understanding of speech long before they learn to talk. At the age of about eight months a baby makes experimental noises and grunts, called experimental vocalisation. It is the way a baby learns how to use and control his vocal cords and the muscles, which work them.

At one year a baby generally says a few words and has some control over the volume, pitch and sound quality of his voice. He clearly understands many simple, familiar words, even though his own speech may be limited to 'Mummy', 'Dada' and 'Tata'.

In the second year of life a baby's speech development is generally slow. This is because he has so many other things to master, such as learning to walk, climb, feed and partly dress himself. By the second birthday, most children speak at least five words, and in some the vocabulary may have reached 100 words or more, although they use no more than three or four words to make a sentence.

As with other milestones, the family environment probably has more influence than any other factor on the development of a child who is in the normal range of intelligence. The development of speech in a child aged between two and five years greatly depends on the opportunities the child has for conversation.

If an infant does not get the opportunity to make conversation, he still chatters away to himself, but his vocabulary does not expand. If your child is told stories each day, he will have a much greater chance of expanding his vocabulary than a child who is not told stories, or who is told to be quiet when he wants to talk.

An intelligent three-year-old may know more than 100 words, and that will be sufficient to enable him to ask more than 200 questions and speak several thousand words in a day.

A five-year-old child can, in nearly all cases, pronounce words, tell a coherent story, recognise emotions such as happiness and jealousy, and describe the shape, colour and texture of things.

If a child seems very awkward in talking, this in itself is no cause for worry. Even so, it is worth consulting a doctor, if a child has not begun to talk by his second year, to see if there is any disorder.

One important physical milestone will be when your baby's teeth start to come through. Although this might not seem like a developmental step, teeth are essential to your baby's learning to chew solid food and to speak properly.

Movement

All movement commences with the acquisition of head control. Your child can sit up, stand up or crawl only with being able to control the position of his head. Development of any kind proceeds from head to toe.

Initially, your baby's movements appear jerky and uncontrolled. A newborn may move his arms, legs, hands and feet when all he wants to do is smile. But gradually over the next three years his movements become refined, becoming more and more specific to match the task in hand.

Crawling, though clever, is what the baby learns first. It may be a clumsy way to get around, but he has first to learn balance and coordination, and acquire self-confidence, before he starts to walk or run.

Hearing and Vision

Hearing is essential to the development of speech. A newborn baby is startled by some sounds, but can be soothed by the reassuring tone of his mother's voice. In time, usually by the age of three months, a baby may recognise the voice as his mother's. After this a baby begins to associate sounds with objects, and to develop the ability to tell from which direction the sounds come. By 9 months the imitation of speech sounds begins, and at 18 months or even earlier the first words are uttered.

If a child is deaf, his intellectual development may suffer because he cannot imitate meaningful human sounds. Such impairment diminishes one of the main functions of hearing: the capacity to communicate through language.

There are various clues you can look for very early on that indicate normal hearing: does he turn towards the location of the sound, or respond to your voice by turning or smiling, for instance?

A newborn baby's view of the world is blurred and meaningless. As he grows older, he learns to recognise what he sees. As a toddler his visual sense is now becoming highly sharper. He now knows the colours and shapes and can identify them. He can now do simple jigsaw puzzles, and fit a square into a square shape, a triangular piece into a triangular slot, etc. In a picture puzzle he is able to spot out certain objects.

Manipulation

With the dexterity of all his fingers, the child can manually perform all easy tasks, and some delicate ones too. He will know how to open a door, turning the doorknob. He can play with simple interlocking toys, and even manipulate children's scissors, a very complicated task for a toddler. He can hold a pencil or a paintbrush and use them if he is taught to do so.

Intelligence and Learning

A child's intelligence is mainly inherited from his parents, and the parents' intelligence is usually a guide to the child's. However, parents of very high or low intelligence usually have children who are nearer average than they are themselves.

Children brought up at home, with all that this means in terms of loving care, are more advanced by the age of six months than are children brought up in an impersonal institution, and this trend often continues into the school years. Some parents teach their children counting games, and, later, word games. Many doctors believe that in spite of a poor start, a poor child from deprived environment often catches up in later life.

Do not expect too much too early. A baby's central nervous system is only partly developed at birth. It grows in size and complexity until it is 90 per cent of adult size at five years. This is why a baby cannot be lavatory-trained much before the age of 18 months, and a two-year-old has not sufficient muscular coordination to ride a tricycle.

The baby's nervous system must develop before he can walk, talk or have simple understanding. All normal children master these skills at about the same age – whether or not their parents spend hours teaching them – because the skills are a part of instinctive behaviour.

Boys and girls have different strengths and will develop differently. The pace of development, be it physical, intellectual or social, is affected by many things, and gender is one of them.

While girls do better at language-based skills, like talking, reading or writing, boys begin to talk at a later stage and more prone to language disorders. Girls tend to be more sociable and more interested in people than things, and are easier to get on with and cope better with stress. Boys, on the other hand, tend to be less sociable and more interested in objects than in people, and are more vulnerable to stress; they are more likely to have behavioural problem. They are also more aggressive and rebellious, and get better at jumping, running and throwing, after the preschool years.

Girls do better at jumping, hopping and balance in the pre-school years. They grow faster and are more predictable and regular in their growth patterns which boys are more likely to grow in sudden spurts.

Sociability

Babies bring a lot of joy into the world and all those near and dear to them receive a lot of pleasure from them. Babies too receive so much love from the outset from everyone around them. This is a mutual give and take. Hence, we must remember that we must respond to their need for affection.

Babies imitate us and will respond to a human voice from birth. So you must talk to your baby from the day he is born, never mind if he cannot hear or respond to your voice initially. You can influence your child in the way you carry yourself, and the way you interact with others. An independent and determined child will try new movements earlier than a reticent one, and a sociable child will seek social contact and communication with others. He will also develop speech earlier than other children.

Your child is blessed with sociability, activity and emotion. His sociability depends on the extent to which he seeks out and enjoys contact with other people. His activity is his prowess at, and enjoyment of, movement and energy, while his emotion is his tendency to mood swings. If one of these traits is prominent, try to encourage your child in developing his other two traits.

Good Environment

In the early months your baby will not be aware of his surroundings, but as the days go by, he gradually starts interacting with his surrounding. To have a stimulating environment, be sure to surround your baby in the first six months with a large variety of sights, sounds, smells and textures. His intellectual and emotional development should be given a chance to flower by providing him with different experiences.

It would be nice to have a special area for your child's activities, for example, a sand pit, or a place where children can amuse themselves with messy activities like painting or water games. A corner of your child's room can be used for arranging all the toys, or for him to play with messy toys. Choose toys that provide education.

Teaching Your Child

Your role as a teacher should come to you naturally and without effort. A child is always curious, and likes to learn new things. So make the experience fun and mutually rewarding. Utilise all opportunities that you get to teach your child colours, shapes, textures, opposites, etc. You can tell him stories with a moral.

Teaching should not be a formal process, with its rigid rules and aims. Let it be a fun way of learning for your child. Encourage your child to be curious so that he experiments with his ideas and anything novel that he comes across. Introduce new ideas and answer all his queries. Always praise him at every stage so that the learning process becomes a natural way of experience, and also gives your child pleasure. This will encourage him to repeat the experience over and over with you.

When your baby takes his first steps, stay close to him, especially when he walks and creeps upstairs. If the floor is slippery, do not give him shoes, unless he goes outside. Let him have a lot of space around for his walking attempts. Try to remove furniture with sharp edges from his path. Put safety gates to the top and bottom of your stairs, making sure that they have vertical bars and not horizontal bars over which he may otherwise climb. Keep all unsafe and poisonous things out of his reach.

It will be fun to help your baby in his attempt to walk, initially to move on his belly , then crawl, before sitting and learning to stand up. When he starts walking, give him a large soft ball that he can learn to kick. This will also give him balancing skills. He will also enjoy ball games, toys on wheels, and games that involve hopping, jumping or climbing. Encourage him in his new skills, build up his confidence, and help him to handle new skills that are difficult at first. A small tricycle can be used indoor as well as out, and this will improve your child's muscle strength and coordination. Indoor, he can play and jump or somersault on a foam rubber or mattress.

Encouraging Skills

Encourage your child's interest in dressing himself by letting him choose the clothes he is to wear. Doing up buttons develops his finger skills. Putting on socks and shoes might still be tricky for a two-year-old, but if he wants to do so, give him the chance to do it; ultimately you will put them on correctly for him. By encouraging his dressing ability, he will soon be able to put on and take off underwear, trousers, knickers, shirts, and so on.

Washing and drying his hands will be something that he may like doing, so encourage him in this. He should now be able to turn over pages without tearing them, so give him plenty of books with colourful pictures. Give him building blocks that need pressing and fitting together, for this will help him develop the small movements of his hands. Very gradually you can introduce simple jigsaw puzzles made of large pieces, or help him thread large beads on to a piece of string.

Teach your child colours. Give him crayons and drawing material. As he draws and fills it with colours, he will gradually be able to identify the colours. Likewise, he can learn to draw and identify various shapes.

Mental Development

Your baby is born with certain number of cells, and as his brain doubles in weight by 12 months, there is growth development of connections between the different cells used in thinking. Your baby points to an object, reaches for it, picks it up, puts it into his mouth, chews it, tastes it – he has used it by train connections and slotted it all into his memory.

Very few children are retarded, and equally few are especially gifted. Never push your child: accept him for who he is, and give him opportunities to develop his talents.

All children have some creative ability, and developing this is very important. Just as you consider teaching him letters of the alphabet and numbers as important, likewise encourage him with his talents. Try to stimulate these creative abilities by pointing out things happening around him, show him pictures, flowers, animals, colours, and smells. Tell him stories so that his imaginative skills improve.

Reasoning

With your child becoming more creative and imaginative, he starts applying all that he has absorbed so far to a given situation. This new ability to think, create and imagine gives him a new perception of the world.

Now he no longer is interested in the things that caught his interests at first. He starts exploring new horizons, and his experience grows. He is constantly gathering information and asking a lot of questions, as his curiosity gets the better of him. He might enjoy using the brooms and mops, while you are working with them, for he becomes very interested in how things work.

By the time your child is three years old, he already has an interest in his own gender, and in this way he is different from the opposite sex. He will begin to express interest in physiological differences between the genders, and in boys' and girls' postures for urinating. He makes no distinctions between genders at play and realises that people touch out of friendship as well as out of love.

He begins to show interest in babies, and wants his family to have one. He will begin to question from where the baby comes or whether the baby will play with him. You must be as frank and honest as possible so that his trust in you is not undermined.

17

CARE OF CHILD'S HEALTH

Most parents know when their child is sickening for something, even though it is difficult to know what precisely is wrong. A child may need special care and attention because of a chronic condition, such as asthma, a learning disorder, or he may have continuous bouts of vomiting. Early identification of special needs is very essential, so the more informed you are, the more you can do for him. First aid is an essential skill for all parents.

When your child is pale, restless, off his food and rather weary, you must realise he is falling ill. You must monitor closely his temperature, appetite and breathing rate.

When to Call the Doctor

When you are not sure what your child is ailing from, you can call a doctor or take your child to the clinic.

The normal body temperature is 98.4° F. If your child's temperature rises above 100.4° F he has a fever, and this is when you should call your doctor. If a stiff neck and a rash accompany the fever, then he could be heading for meningitis, so consult your doctor urgently. When checking his temperature, don't put the thermometer in his mouth at least until he is seven years old. Place the thermometer bulb in his armpit and fold his arm over his chest; hold in place for about three minutes before you remove it and note that reading.

Diarrhoea, loose, watery bowel movements, is a matter of concern in babies and young children as it can lead to dehydration. It could mean that the intestines are inflamed and irritable, needing a doctor's care immediately.

If your child vomits intermittently during a six-hour period, especially if he has diarrhoea or fever also, then consult your doctor at once. The cause for vomiting could be gastroenteritis or food that does not suit; sometimes it could be something more serious and your doctor should be able to diagnose it.

If your child complains of headache, he must see a doctor. It can be serious if he has bumped his head or if the headache comes on a few hours after the head injury, or if there is blurred vision, nausea, dizziness or stomach pain, especially on the lower right side of the abdomen.

Difficulty in breathing is a medical emergency and requires immediate attention. You will note that with laboured breathing your child's ribs are drawn in sharply each time he takes a breath. If his lips turn blue then it is a case of extreme emergency, so call for an ambulance, or admit him in a hospital at once.

Sudden changes in appetite may indicate underlying illness, especially if he has a fever, even a mild one. If he continues to refuse food even for a day and seems lethargic, your doctor should be alerted.

Apart from the treatment that your doctor recommends, your child must be made to feel comfortable while he is ill. Air his room and bed at least once a day. If he is vomiting, keep a bowl near his bed. If he has a running nose, keep a box of tissues nearby.

Give him small meals frequently for he may not be able to eat much at one time. Do not insist if he does not feel like eating, but do encourage him to drink lots of fluid. If he has high fever, sponge him down with cold water. Give him liquid paracetamol for pain relief.

When your child is unwell, do not follow any rigid rules, but use your common sense and listen to the demands of the situation. It would help if you try to hide your anxiety from your child.

When illness sets in, your child would like to be in bed and probably sleep a lot. As his health improves, he will still need bed rest, but he will want to be up and about, and he may want to play. The best way to deal with such a situation would be for you to either make him lie down on a sofa near you, or you can make him sit for a while near you if you are busy with your chores. If you are relatively free, then spend some time with him as he is lying on his bed, occupying him with stories. Don't insist that he should go to bed just because he is ill, but because he is tired. Don't just leave him alone for long. Make sure that you visit him at regular intervals. If he is awake, after a rest, you can stay with him and play a game or do a puzzle with him.

If your child is suffering from diarrhoea or vomiting, or is just having fever, it is important that he drinks a lot of liquids, as he will be dehydrated and needs to replenish lost fluids. The recommended fluid intake for a child with fever is 100-150 ml per kg of body weight per day, which is equal to 1 litre per day for a child weighing 9 kgs.

Encourage your child to drink by leaving his favourite drink at his bedside. Do not give sugar, fizzy or aerated drinks like cola. You can tempt him to drink it by putting it in a glass that is especially appealing and by giving him bent straws to drink with.

You can indulge your child completely when he is ill. Relax all rules and let him play whatever games he wants to, even if earlier you had not allowed them in bed. When he is not resting, spend time talking to him and playing games with him. If he wants to engage himself with painting, a messy job, spread an oilcloth or just an old sheet of polythene or thick cotton over the bed. If it is possible, he can lie down in front of the television to watch his favourite cartoons, which will keep him entertained as well as keep him in one place. If his friends want to visit him, let them join him, unless your child has an infectious disease. Don't allow the friends to stay too long for your child to become very tired. If he has fever, discourage your child from running around.

If your child has vomiting distress, try to make him as uncomfortable as possible. Get him to sit up in bed, and make sure there is a bowl or a basin within reach, so that he doesn't have to run to the toilet. If he is being sick, hold his head and comfort him. Afterwards, help him to clean his teeth, and give him a peppermint to suck to remove the obnoxious taste.

When your child has not vomited for a few hours, and he is feeling hungry, give him bland foods, but don't force him to eat if he dislikes it. He can drink something that he likes, except aerated drinks. In fact, giving him more fluids is more important than eating. Let him take lots of water to which is added a teaspoon of salt and four teaspoons of glucose per 500 ml to replace salts and minerals. Avoid giving him milk, but give him fresh fruit juice instead.

If the fever lasts for more than 24 hours, or if there are other symptoms also like vomiting or a rash or diarrhoea, call a doctor. If the temperature is about 100.4^0 F, then it could be serious.

Cool your child down by removing his clothes and making him lie on the bed. Sponge him all over with tepid water, and keep taking his temperature until it has stabilised at 100.4^0 F. Never use cold water to sponge him since this causes the blood vessels to constrict and the temperature to increase. Cover him with a light cotton sheet and check his temperature every minute to see that it does not go up again. Changing the sheets on the bed frequently will help your child to keep comfortable. It is still important that he drinks lots of fluid, as he will be sweating a lot.

Some babies can have convulsions when they have a high temperature due to a viral infection. This sort of convulsion is quite common in children aged six months to four years old. This condition is known as febrile convulsion.

When a child has convulsions, the muscles of his body twitch involuntarily due to a temporary abnormality in brain function. Other symptoms possibly could be loss of consciousness, loss of bladder and bowel control, rhythmic jerking of the limbs, with sleepiness and confusion on coming round. There should be a clear space around him so that he does not hurt himself. Wait until his body has stopped jerking, and then place him in the recovery position.

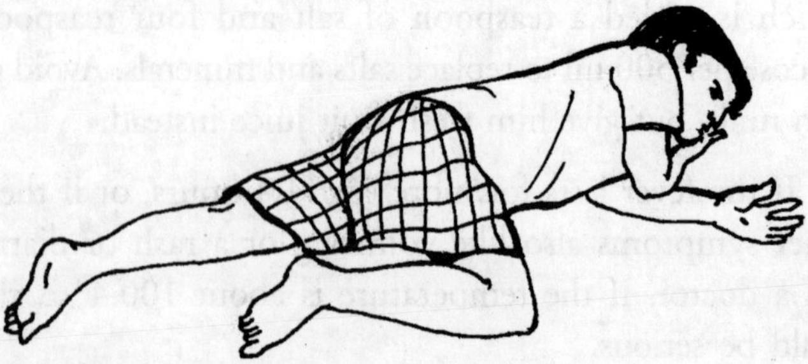

Sponge your child with tepid (never cold) water to reduce his temperature. Do not leave him alone, restrain him or put anything in his mouth. Call a doctor as soon as your child has come round. If the convulsions last more than 15 minutes, call an ambulance.

18

TREATING COMMON CHILDHOOD ILLNESSES

A child's immune system takes time to develop, and hence, any illness in him is different from, and more serious than the same illness in an adult. Prompt action should be taken if your child falls ill.

Ears

Infections of the ear are quite common in children as their Eustachian tube (the tube that connects the middle ear to the pharynx at the back of the throat) are short. So any infection can rise quickly to the middle ear.

Otitis Media

This is a serious form of infection of the middle ear, caused by germs carried to the ear through the Eustachian tube from the throat when the victim has infected tonsils, sore throat, adenoids, sinusitis or a bad cold. Middle ear infection usually produces severe earache, a feeling of pressure in the ear, and sometimes, if the ear-drum ruptures, a discharge from the ear. If not treated, it can result in deafness or more serious complications. Do not attempt home treatment of an ear infection, but consult a doctor, who can prescribe drugs to clear it up.

Glue Ear

When your child suffers from tonsillitis, or has repeated infections of the middle ear, a jelly-like fluid accumulates in the middle ear. Since the fluid cannot drain away through the Eustachian tube, it becomes glue-like and obstructs hearing, for the sounds are not being transmitted across the middle ear to the inner ear, where they are actually heard. This condition should be attended to at once, else your child could be slow to speak and learn.

Glue ear generally does not cause any earache, but your child will have only partial hearing, and he may feel fullness deep in his ear. He may sleep with his mouth open, he may snore while sleeping, and speak with a nasal twang.

The treatment would be with antibiotics and vasoconstrictor drugs to clear the infection and allow the fluid to drain. Only in very acute cases is a minor operation necessary, which involves inserting a plastic tube to drain off the mucus through the eardrum.

Throat

Babies under one year rarely have throat infections. Tonsillitis and adenitis are common in children who have just started school and are being exposed to a new range of bacteria.

Sore Throat

A sore may be a part of the body's early warning system – a symptom that the throat is being invaded by germs. The throat never becomes sore of its own accord – something makes it sore. That something, whether a virus or bacteria, could be dangerous if it is not treated. Normally, the infection in children is due to infection by a bacterium such as streptococcus, or a virus such as the cold or flu viruses.

Your child may have difficulty in swallowing due to a sore throat. There could be inflammation or enlarged red tonsils. Give him lots of drinks, and give him soft semi-solid or liquid food if he finds it difficult to swallow. Your doctor may prescribe an antibiotic if there is bacterial infection or tonsillitis.

Tonsillitis and Swollen Adenoids

Tonsillitis is the most common throat disease among children. It usually strikes between the ages of four and eight years, and is often associated with adenoid trouble.

Tonsils are a pair of flat, oval masses of tissue that lie one on each side of the entrance to the throat. Your child may complain of sore throat, and find swallowing difficult. At first the child's tonsils are red and swollen, and there may be white spots on the tonsils. In addition, the tongue may be furred, and there may be vomiting or diarrhoea, followed by a fever with a temperature of up to 105^0 F. The glands in his neck may be swollen and his breath might smell. If the adenoids too are swollen, his speech may sound nasal.

Your doctor may take a throat swab and examine your child's ears and glands. Appropriate antibiotics are prescribed for bacterial tonsillitis. If his tonsils become repeatedly infected, the doctor may advise that they be removed surgically by an operation called tonsillectomy. Often the surgeon also removes the child's adenoids at the same time, if they are diseased.

Skin

Most disorders that directly affect the skin cause some sort of eruption, such as swelling, blistering, redness, spots, pimples, a rash or hard lumps. Childhood skin complaints may be caused by an infection, an allergy or response to very high or low temperatures. Most of them are minor, and can be easily treated. Rashes are accompanied by a variety of complaints some of which can be serious. So consult your doctor.

Infantile Eczema

This can occur with no obvious cause. It is particularly trying for infants, who become restless and irritable. Many such children have a family history of allergic conditions such as eczema, or asthma. The skin gets inflamed, triggered by an allergy or an infection. Occasionally it is simply a reaction to stress. Atopic eczema is the type that usually affects children. This appears between two and 18 months of age, typically occurring on the face, hands, neck, ankles, and in the knee and elbow creases. Seborrhoeic dermatitis (the outermost layer of dead cells on the skin coming off in scales or flakes) affects the children, occurring on the scalp, eyelids and ears, around the nose, in the ear canal and groin.

Atopic eczema causes the skin to be raw, dry, scaly, red and itchy, with small white blisters, like rice grains, which burst and weep if scratched. Seborrhoeic eczema is less itchy. Itchiness is the most irritating and troublesome symptom of eczema, causing severe scratching and sleeplessness.

Your doctor may prescribe an anti-inflammatory cream and antihistamines to curb itching and cure any allergy. An infected skin will need antibiotics. Keep contact with the water to the minimum, and add baby oil in the bath before your child has his bath. Do not use soap, and ensure that the clothes are thoroughly rinsed, with no residue of washing detergent or fabric conditioner. Minimise your child's contact with potential allergens. Keep his fingernails short so that he cannot scratch and damage the skin. Use emollient cream on his skin.

Colds and Coughs

Children develop immunity to specific viruses, as they grow older. So in the earlier years they are susceptible to infections with cold or flu viruses. There are about 200 cold viruses producing similar symptoms, but your child will never get the same virus twice.

Common Cold

Colds are more frequent when your child starts attending play school, as he will be exposed to lots of new viruses. Colds are not serious unless your child is very young, or a complication such as bronchitis sets in.

The symptoms usually appear 19-48 hours after infection. They include a stuffy or running nose, headache and cough. There may be a feeling of chilliness, the sensations of smell and taste may become less acute, and the child may develop a slight fever. He may also suffer from a general feeling of listlessness and discomfort. As the disorder develops, there may be a sore throat, varying from mild to severe, and a cough. It may last from a couple of days to a couple of weeks.

There is no cure for the common cold, though the symptoms can be treated, but not the virus itself. Unless a secondary infection like sinusitis or bronchitis appears for which the doctor will prescribe antibiotics, home remedies will suffice. A light diet with plenty of fluids should be given to your child. Encourage him to blow his nose frequently, showing him how to clear each nostril at a time. You can apply petroleum jelly to his nostril and chapstick for his lips if they become sore or chopped. If congestion is severe, with nostrils clogged, ensure that he sleeps with his head propped up with pillows, and try applying a menthol rub to his chest.

Your doctor may prescribe nose drops if a blocked nose interferes with sleeping or eating. Liquid paracetamol reduces the temperature, and eases aches and pains. Get your child to inhale dissolved menthol crystals in boiling water. Cover his head with a towel to keep in the menthol vapours.

Coughs

A cough is a protective reflex, which tries to rid the windpipe or the bronchial tubes of anything that is blocking or irritating them. Inhaled dust–or an object such as a fruit pip or a peanut–causes a bout of coughing. More often mucus from the lungs or from the nasal passages irritates the windpipe and produces coughing.

When nothing is coughed up and the cough is persistent, its cause may be difficult to determine. Going out in cold weather may bring on a short, dry cough. It may also be caused by influenza, or accompany inflammation of the larynx, tonsils or windpipe.

When children cough, it is most often the sign of common cold or influenza. But it could indicate bronchitis, croup, sore throat, tonsillitis or even earache. In addition, a cough may be early warning sign of measles, whooping cough or an allergy. A child with a persistent cough should see a doctor.

There are two types of cough: a productive cough and a non-productive cough. In a productive cough, phlegm is produced, and in a non-productive one there is no phlegm. The first type has a "wet" sound, while the second is dry and hacking, and both will prevent sleep.

One cause of cough in children is croup. This is an acute respiratory infection. It is most common in winter and the start of summer, and usually occurs first at night. Most cases of croup result from infection by a virus, but a bacterium may also be responsible. The most typical symptom is the sound of croup. The voice becomes hoarse and raspy, and a harsh cough develops. Since the larynx is swollen, there is difficulty in breathing, and for a child this is often terrifying. Fever might be slight or high, depending on the type of croup. In severe cases there may be blueness of the lips. Sticky mucus tends to clog the throat, and the larynx, windpipe and bronchial tubes are infected.

If you suspect that your child has croup or asthma, you must seek medical help at once. If the cough is due to a chronic infection like sinusitis or tonsillitis, they should be treated with medicines prescribed by the doctor. Most other coughs can be treated at home so long as the cough does not disturb your child's sleep.

Your child needs to rest, so discourage him from running around, as this may make him breathless and bring on a coughing fit. Make him lie on his side or stomach at night to prevent mucus running down the throat. To relieve his cough–which is a symptom and not a disease–plenty of hot liquids may be helpful. It is better to give cough expectorant instead of strong cough medicines.

Infectious Diseases

Most infectious diseases are caused by micro-organisms bacterium or virus. The infection can be air-borne or spread via food, water or insects, especially in poor hygienic conditions. There are less chances of this threat with high sanitation, appropriate drugs, and better health and nutrition programmes. Many serious infectious diseases, like smallpox, have been virtually eliminated in developed countries by immunisation. The symptoms of many childhood infectious diseases are similar: rash on the body, fever, general malaise and common cold. A rash on the body accompanied by fever needs to be seen by a doctor. The dangers of such illnesses could be dehydration due to vomiting and refusal to eat and drink, difficulty in breathing due to clogged airways, or febrile convulsions. Some diseases, if left untreated, can lead to complications.

Chickenpox

This is an acute, infectious disease that is caused by a virus and marked by eruptions on the skin. The disease is not considered serious, and generally lasts about two weeks after the first appearance of symptoms.

Chickenpox is very contagious, and the child should be kept away from other people. The disease, known medically as varicella, is among the most common of childhood diseases. It spreads by contact with a person who has it, or by breathing infectious droplets in the air.

The first symptoms appear 10-18 days after exposure. Fever and discomfort are usually mild in children, but more severe in adults. Your child may have no appetite. A rash of small red marks appears on his back and chest, and spreads to his face, scalp, arms and elsewhere. After some hours, the marks became blisters; these soon fill with pus, and, finally, they form crusts. In one or two weeks, the crusts drop off. There is a lot of itching during this period.

You must ensure that your child does not scratch, since there is a risk of secondary infection and scarring. Cut his fingernail short, and make sure that his hands are kept clean. Get him to take baths frequently when the fever is gone, to keep his skin clean. The itching may be relieved by applications of calamine lotion, or by taking a cold bath containing several handfuls of starch. An antihistamine, prescribed by the doctor, can also be helpful. He may also prescribe an anti-infective cream.

In very rare cases, chickenpox may lead to encephalitis (inflammation of the brain) and, if aspirin is taken, Reye's syndrome, a serious illness whose symptoms are nausea, vomiting, noticeable lethargy and fever. One attack of chickenpox normally gives immunity for life.

German Measles

This is the common name for rubella, an infectious disease common in childhood. It is also known as the 'three-day-measles'. Like the seven-day measles (rubeala), this is a contagious virus disease characterised by a pink rash, starting behind the ears, and spreading to the face, neck and body. One attack generally gives immunity for life.

The symptoms of rubella are mild. There may be fever and tenderness in the lymph modes at the back of the neck. Your child may not know he has any illness until a rash appears two or three weeks after exposure to the disease.

The rash disappears after one to three days, and recovery occurs without any specific treatment.

If a woman contracts German measles during the first three months of pregnancy; the chances are quite high that the baby will have serious birth defects. Therefore pregnant woman should not be exposed to the infected person in this case, may be her own child. The child with the disease has a slight risk of encephalitis (inflammation of the brain).

Mumps

This is an acute, contagious disease that generally affects children between the ages of five and 15. A virus transmitted in the saliva of an infected person causes it. The symptoms appear two or three weeks after exposure. One attack usually, but not always, gives immunity for life.

Swelling of the face and neck is the most typical symptom of mumps. Swelling of the inflamed parotid gland, a saliva-secreting gland below the ear, produces this. Sometimes, the nearby sub-maxillary gland is also affected. The swelling usually begins on one side, and may appear on the other in a day or two. The child has a headache, and fever may be as high as 104^0 F. Sometimes there is vomiting, but in mild cases hardly any of these symptoms appear.

Give your child plenty to drink. If he has fever, he should stay in bed until it subsides. If he has no fever, keep him at home until the swelling comes down.

Less common symptoms are painful testicles in boys and swollen ovaries in girls. Only some areas of the testicles are affected, and so it is very rare for infertility or sterility to follow an attack of mumps.

Measles

This is a contagious disease, generally of childhood, caused by a virus. Its most prominent symptom is a pink rash, which appears on the face, neck and body. The first symptoms of the disease resemble those of a cold; sore eyes, sneezing, coughing and a running nose. The body temperature rises, occasionally reaching as much as 106^0 F by the fourth day. The rash, consisting of many small red spots, appears from three to five days after the onset of other symptoms and lasts for four to seven days. It generally starts behind the ears and on the forehead, and spreads rapidly, often covering the entire body. The fever spikes with appearance of rash. A doctor can diagnose measles by looking for Koplik's spots, white-centred red spots in the mouth, inside the cheeks, which appear a day or two before the rash.

Complete recovery from measles generally occurs within two to four weeks, unless there are complications. A child with measles can easily catch other infections, from the common cold to pneumonia, and so careful convalescence is important.

The child should be isolated in a well ventilated room, not merely to prevent others from catching the disease, but also to protect him from secondary infections. His eyes may be sensitive to bright light, and drawing the six-room curtains may help. He should be kept in bed until his temperature returns to normal, and then allowed to get up when he wants to, if he seems well enough.

Babies should be vaccinated against measles when they are about nine months old, although vaccination is just as effective in older children. A single injection produces immunity, probably for life.

Whooping Cough

This is an acute, very contagious disease of the bronchial tubes and the upper-respiratory passages. It is primarily a disease of childhood, generally attacking children under 10 years of age, and is especially dangerous in early infancy. Few children get whooping cough more than once.

The incubation period cough is seven to 14 days. The early stage, which lasts for a week or two, is much like a heavy cold, with some fever and a persistent cough. At this time, the disease may escape diagnosis. Then the cough grows worse, and the child begins to 'whoop' (the sound of the cough is more like a bark than a whoop). This stage lasts up to four weeks from the start of the illness, and then gradually subsides. During this period, the disease is still contagious.

The child should be kept in bed while the fever lasts. He should have plenty of fresh air, as it seems to lessen the severity of the coughing. A well-balanced, plentiful diet is important during whooping cough to prevent undue loss of weight. If vomiting occurs after coughing spells, small amounts of food at frequent intervals may help. Antibiotics such as erythromycin can shorten the duration of the disease, if given early.

A vaccine against whooping cough is usually given to infants as young as six weeks, followed by two more injections at monthly intervals. It is commonly combined with tetanus and diphtheria vaccines.

Meningitis

This is inflammation of the meninges, the membranes covering the brain and spinal cord. It can attack people of all ages, but is most common in children. It is always a serious illness, and is generally caused by any of several bacteria, such as meningococus and those that cause pneumonia and tuberculosis.

Tests have to be conducted in the laboratory to distinguish between bacterial and virus meningitis, since the symptoms of both diseases are often the same. They begin with a severe headache, high fever, vomiting, and often stiffness of the neck and back muscles. The child needs hospitalisation. Intravenous antibiotics are used for bacterial meningitis, and pain-killing drugs relieve the symptoms of viral meningitis.

In children under two, there may be a bulging fontanelle, the soft areas on a baby's head where the skull bone has not fused. In meningococus meningitis, a purple rash that does not disappear on pressure may cover most of the body. Your child should be taken straight to hospital, for this is potentially dangerous.

Diphtheria

This is an acute, contagious disease caused by a bacteria. The diphtheria infection usually first lodges in the upper respiratory tract, producing symptoms like those of the common cold, such as sore throat, fever, general discomfort and weakness. A gray membrane forms in the throat, and constricting forms in the throat, constricting the air passages.

As the bacillus multiplies, it produces a powerful toxin, which circulates throughout the system. The patient appears very weak and sick. The heart muscles and the nerves, especially the cranial nerves, may be involved. Swallowing is difficult, vision is disturbed, and the pulse is weak. Untreated diphtheria is often fatal.

Prompt administration of antitoxin, penicillin, and absolute rest in bed are necessary for recovery. Immunisation has made this disease rare in more countries.

Scarlet Fever

This is an infectious disease marked by fever, sore throat, and a widespread, bright red rash. It is caused by streptococcus bacterium, and develops only in people who are susceptible to the toxin produced in the body by the streptococci. It is typically a disease of childhood, but may also occur in adults.

Once a dreaded disease that lasted for several weeks, it has become less serious now as it can now easily be treated with penicillin or other antibiotics.

Scarlet fever usually begins with nausea, vomiting and headache. There is fever, and the skin is hot and dry. In a day or so, a rash breaks out; the tongue is coated and turns a brilliant red. After about a week the rash fades, and the skin starts to peel. By this time, the disease is no longer contagious. The doctor may wish to examine the patient's urine to ensure that the kidney disease (nephritis) has not developed.

Other Disorders

Besides the diseases mentioned above, children might be affected by other disorders. Chest infections, such as bronchitis and pneumonia, usually follow a common cold or sore throat. Coughing follow a common cold or sore throat. Coughing and wheezing may occur, and some children develop asthma. Children can also get influenza.

Allergic Disorders

Asthma – difficulty in breathing caused by narrowing of the air passages to the lungs – is common in childhood. It may be triggered off by bronchitis or be caused by an allergy to pollen or dust. In some children, emotional stress plays a part. Skin conditions, such as eczema, may be due to irritation from a detergent or an allergic reaction to a food or a particular fabric.

Abdominal Pains

Sudden pain in a child's abdomen – the typical stomach ache – is nearly always caused by overeating food that is too rich, or eating when excited. But if the pain lasts for more than an hour, if it is accompanied by vomiting, or if the child also passes blood-stained urine or faeces, a doctor should be consulted. Possible causes are appendicitis and a rare blockage of intestines.

Senses Defects

Unless disorders of the senses or nervous system are recognised and treated early, a child's development and education can be seriously impaired. Among the most common are poor eyesight, and deafness or partial deafness, which account for many cases of so-called backwardness in children. More obvious is a squint, which must receive treatment if the child's eyesight is not to be permanently damaged.

Growth Disorders

A doctor should see any child who fails to gain weight at a normal rate, even though apparently healthy. Retarded growth is rare, and is generally caused by a disorder of the pituitary gland. A disorder of the same gland causes excessive growth, and both need specialist treatment. Poor nutrition, such as deficiency of essential vitamins, may cause conditions such as rickets. In underdeveloped countries, lack of proper food leads to malnutrition and disorders such as kwashiorkor.

Mental Disorders

True mental retardation is usually present from birth (congenital), and no treatment is possible; but a rare disorder of brain chemistry, such as phenylketonuria, may be responsible. Early diagnosis ensures that such chemical conditions can be successfully treated.

Behavioural disorders, such as bed-wetting, truancy and stealing, can often be traced to emotional insecurely or stress. Depression and psychosis, such as infantile schizophrenia, do occur in children, but they are rare.

Kwashiorkor

This is a protein deficiency disease, common in parts of Africa, occurring in infants after weaning. The weaned child gets more carbohydrates than protein, and protein is needed for the rapid growth. This usually occurs in an infant's age one to three years.

Lack of growth, anorexia, gastro-intestinal ailments, nausea and diarrhoea are the common symptoms. Digestion also becomes poor, and there is swelling in the face and limbs. The child's hair turns yellowish and falls off in patches. The skin too starts flaking and peeling off. Dis-pigmentation and hyper-pigmentation are common. The liver may become tender and enlarged. The child becomes listless, irritable, apathetic and sluggish in movements and thinking.

Protein-rich food is a must for the infant. He also needs to be active, so give him plenty of fresh fruit juices.

Marasmus

This is a disease of infants and young children in which severe wasting occurs because the diet is deficient in protein and calories. Occasionally marasmus follows on attack of gastro-enteritis. It can occur at any age, including adulthood, in times of famine.

In children it is common during the first year of life, and the two constant features are retarded growth and severe wasting of muscles and fat. The children have a wizened, aged look on their faces. Response to treatment is often very slow. The diet should contain good-quality protein, such as that from soya beans or skimmed milk, but the calorie intake is very important and should be raised immediately to the recommended level.

19

CHART OF COMMON PROBLEMS & INFECTIOUS ILLNESSES

All children, however healthy, can become ill. It can seem to be an almost continuous stream of afflictions. We present a guide to the most common.

Illness	Incubation Period	Infections Period	Symptoms
Asthma			Children with Asthma tend to breathe harder. Their breathing is accompanied by a wheezing noise, which is most noticeable when breathing out. The small beathing tubes in the lungs become narrowed; this is caused by tightening of the muscles in the walls of the tubes, the swelling of their lining and the increased production of mucus.
Bronchitis	1-7 days	Two days prior to symptom appearing and two days after	Frequent coughing, laboured breathing, occasionally fever and wheezing.
Chicken Pox	14-21 days	From the day before symptoms first appear until two days after	Itching, pink or red spots covering chest, stomach and back. Spot change quickly to watery blisters and eventually crust. Fever and general discomfort

Common Cold	1-7 days	Two days before symptoms first appear until two days after	Sneezing, stuffed-up running nose, watery eyes, sore throat, probable cough and temperature.
Conjunctivitis	1-2 days	A few days.	Eyes painful and red. Crusty discharge and itchiness.
Croup	2-6 days	Two days before symptoms appear, to about five days after	Racking hoarse cough sounds like barking, coughing mainly at night and possible difficulty in breathing in.
Diphtheria	2-10 days	From the onset of the disease for about four weeks	Sore throat, difficulty in swallowing, high temperature headache, fever. Milder symptoms if previously immunized.
Gastro-enteritis	1-3 days	While any symptoms are present	Vomiting, uneasiness, diarrhoea, stomach cramps, retching and perhaps fever.

Prevention	Treatment
Almost all attacks are allergic reactions caused by exposure to allergens such as grass pollens, house dust mite or pet's furx; it is important to reduce a child's exposure to these. Sudden changes of temperature and hot winds, even exercise, can bring on attacks so prevention can be very difficult.	Consult your doctor. Drugs which open the small breathing tubes relieve attacks. The doctor may prescribe tablets, mixtures or aerosols. Prescribed drugs should be given at the onset of an attack as they will be more effective. Preventative medicines are also available and are generally very effective.
None.	Consult your doctor. He may prescribe penicillin to deal with the infection. If the child has fever make sure he rests. Give plenty of liquids. Inhalations may help him breathe more easily.
None.	Consult your doctor. Trim child's fingernails to help prevent secondary infection from scratching. Calamine lotion will relieve itching, so too will frequent cool baths using medicated soap. Rest is essential. Chicken pox is highly infectious, so keep child's dishes and utensils separate from the rest of the family.

None.	Consult your doctor if you are worried. But treatment generally is straight forward. The child should be given plenty of fluids, kept warm, and have lots of rest. Treat fever. Consulting a doctor is advisable if symptoms persist or become significantly worse. Consult your doctor. Many cases are viral but sometimes antibiotics are helpful.
Careful washing of hands.	Consult your doctor. Many cases are viral but sometimes antibiotics are helpful.
None.	Steam from a kettle or filling the bathroom with steam will relieve the distress. A vaporizer from the chemist will also help. If not, and the child is distressed, go to the hospital. Consult your doctor if the child's condition persists.
Immunization with triple antigen.	Consult your doctor immediately. Diphtheria is a serious disease, highly infectious and dangerous. Your child may need hospital care.
Meticulous hygiene may help.	Gastro-enteritis is caused by a bowel virus infection. Be careful the child does not become dehydrated and give him lots of fluids.

German measles (rubella)	14-21 days	Before rash to four to five days after its apperance	Slight fever, headache, enlarged neck glands, pink rash, usually heaviest on face, neck and upper chest. Running nose, inflamed eyes, painful joints.
Hay fever			Nasal congestion, sneezing, clear nasal discharge and itching of the nose. The eyes can also feel itchy and the ears may feel obstructed.
Hepatitis A Infectious hepatitis	20-30 days	120 days.	Gradual onset of nausea, vomiting, pain on right side of abdomen, dark urine, yellow skin and eyes.
Hepatitis B	3-4 months	120 days.	Gradual appearance of jaundice, dark urine and pale stool.
Influenza (virus flu)	1-4 days	One day before symptoms appear, to seven days after.	Similar to the common cold but with additional symptoms such as severe headache and back-of neck ache, chills fever, body aches and pains, loss of appetite and possible nausea or vomitting
Impetigo (scabby sores)	4-14 days	Two days before sores appear until after scabs heal.	Small red spots quickly changing to blisters which break open leaving pus-filled crusty sores. Also tenderness and sweling of lymph glands and glands in groin, armpit and/or neck.

Measles	10-12 days	Four to five days before rash first appears and up until a week after	General misery, headache, fever, running nose, watery eyes, dry cough. The pink-red rash appears, several days after the onset of the previous symptoms. It starts on forehead, then face and body.
Meningitis	7-10 days.	Depends on the type of bacteria or virus.	Severe headache, usually very stiff at back of neck. Drowsiness, fever, vomitting, refusal to feed, fullness of fontanelle (soft spot on baby's skull), even fits or unconsciousness.
Mumps	14-28 days.	Four to seven days before swelling and until the swelling subsides.	Fever, headache, generally upset and miserable, possible nausea and vomitting, pain or soreness in jaw and in glands below ears, swelling and tenderness of gland below the ear or jaw bone. Usually swelling starts on one side and spreads to the other.

	Vomiting and diarrhoea may mean gastro-enteritis but can also be symptoms of other diseases. Consult your doctor. Antibiotics rarely help.
Serum to immunize against rubella is advisable at 15 months with measles and mumps vaccine.	Consult your doctor. The child needs bed rest, possibly paracetamol for discomfort during the fever period and a light diet. Make sure the child has had no contact with pregnant women (German measles during pregnancy is dangerous for the unborn child).
Reduce the child's exposure to offending substances such as pollens, feathers, house mites, moulds and animals.	Consult your doctor who will probably prescribe medicine.
Gamma globulin for family contacts.	Consult your doctor. Special diet may be necessary until nausea and vomiting stops. Transmission from a child is very unlikely but utensils and dishes should be kept separate.
Vaccine available but not yet recommended for general use.	Long-term effects are possible and your doctor should be consulted. Spread from the chills is unlikely.
Routine immunization for influenza can help. It is not 100 percent effective as there are many different types of flu virus. Consult doctor about immunization early each year.	Consult your doctor. Bed rest is essential. A diet of fluids gradually progressing to solid foods will help. Severe cases of flu may need autibiotics as part of the treatment.

Antiseptic soap for all members of the household.	Prompt attention is essential as this is highly infectious and spreads rapidly. Try to launder child's sheets and clothes seperately to family wash and keep dishes separate. Shorten child's fingernails to prevent reinfection from scratching. Hygiene is important. Keep hands clean and cleanse the skin around the sores with antiseptic several times a day. Impetigo responds rapidly to antibiotics.
Immunization with mumps and rubella at 15-18 months.	This is a very serious disease because of its complications. Consult your doctor. Special care should be taken to prevent complications such as chills or colds developing into pneumonia. Rest in a shaded darkened room is important. A light diet and lots of fluids are also important.
Antibiotics used in prevention of spread to contacts (usually only family contacts).	Consult your doctor immediately. Very urgent hospitalisation and treatment by antibiotics.
An effective vaccine is available and is given as a combination dose.	Consult your doctor. Mumps is an actue contagious disease, caused by a virus and transmitted in the saliva of an infected.

Pneumonia	2-14 days	Varies.	Coughing, cold and flu symptoms, some pain in chest, lack of appetite, thirst. Usually follows a cold or bronchitis.
Polio	7-14 days	Two to seven days after first symptoms appear.	Fever, headache, numbness, paralysis.
Ringworm (tinea)	10-15 days	Two days before first symptom and then until the infection has cleared.	A small round scaly patch in hair, gradually enlarging, causing hair to become brittle and break, leaving a small bald patch. Ringworm on skin is usually a round or oval eruption which spreads out, becoming scaly and reddened. The centre clears leaving a typical ring shape. Severe inflammation and crusting can develop if the infection is severe.
Roseola	10-14 days	Varies	Sudden fever lasting several days. After fever disappears, a rash of flat or raised spots appears on chest, stomach and back and spreads over the body. Often confused with German measles but the initial fever and high temperature make it easily identifiable. Child not usually very sick.
Scarlet fever	1-5 days	Until throat swab is negative (usually four weeks).	Is rare these days. Painful throat, fever, nausea, vomiting. Within three days a fine rash appears on neck, armpit and groin then spreads over rest of body.

Staphylo-coccal infection	2-5 days	While symptoms present.	Boils, carbuncles, pink, tender infected eruptions Sheeding of skin like a burn in infants under 6 months.
Strepto-coccal throat	2-5 days	A few days before the onset, to the end of symptoms.	Painful throat, fever, nausea, vomitting, swollen, tender neck glands. This precedes scarlet fever.
Tonsillitis	2-5 days	Tonsillitis is not normally infectious from child to child.	A sore throat, fever, swollen neck glands, abdominal pain and difficulty swallowing and eating.
Whooping cough	5-21 days	From the onset of symptoms for four weeks	Begins like a cold. After three weeks spasm of coughing occur until the child almost chokes for breath and becomes purple in the face. Vomiting may follow. May be a clear, running discharge from child's nose.
Worms		While worms are present	Probably no symptoms but perhaps pains in abdomen, irritability, itchy bottom, disturbed sleep.

Sles and rubella vaccine at the age of 15-18 months.	For this reason keep the patient's utensils and dishes separate from the rest of the family's. The child needs rest in bed until fever abates. Diet should be light and paracetamol may be needed. Complications may occur if the child is older.
None.	Consult your doctor immediately. Usually a course of antibiotics is given. Rest, light diet with fluids and warmth is essential. Vaporisers may be necessary.
Sabin vaccine given with the Triple Antigen in the first 6 months of life.	Consult your doctor immediately. Polio should be treated at once. Hospitalisation of the child is usually necessary.
Good hygiene	Ringworm is a fungus infection which spreads rapidly by touching infected towels, sheets, combs or clothing. Wash these separately from the rest of the family's. Consult your doctor immediately to prevent the infection spreading over the body. Frequent and thorough cleaning is essential. Trim child's nails to help prevent scratching and re infection.
None.	Mainly affects children under 3 years. There are no complications apart from a risk of convulsions if fever is high. If worried call your doctor. Generally no special teatment is needed and the disease is usually mild in attack.

Preventive pencillin for family contacts.	This can be a serious disease. Consult your doctor. The child needs plenty of rest and fluid. Antibiotics help recovery.
Antispetic soap for family contact plus good hygiene.	Boils and carbuncles are extremely painful. The staphylococcus germ enters the hair follicle and causes an eruption. More likely to occur if child is run down. They are infectious so the area should be kept scupulously clean. It takes three or four days for a boil to come to a head and burst. Don't squeeze them, let them run their course. If a crop develops see a doctor. Antibiotics may be necessary.
Preventive penicillin.	Consult your doctor. Can develop into other, serious illnesses such as rheumatic fever or kidney inflammation. Antibiotics will probably be given. Make sure child rests and drinks plenty of fluid.
None.	Consult your doctor, he will control the fever. Antibiotics are usually prescribed; fluids and a soft diet are part of the treatment. Recurrences are common. Tonsils are normally only removed if they are chronically infected and affect speech or breathing.

Triple antigen immunization.	This is one of the most serious infectious fevers. Consult your doctor immediately. Middle ear infection and broncho-pneumona are the most common complications of whooping cough. The severity of coughing can cause complications. Antibiotics are used. Frequent small meals reduce the risk of vomiting.
Good hygiene including hand washing before meals and after going to the toilet.	Medicines to treat various types of worms are available at the chemist. Or your doctor can prescribe one. Threadworms are the most common. These look like little white threads and can be seen in the rectum area. Children also contact hook or round worms. Cut child's nails so they are less likely to trap worm eggs. Give child and family, medicine to prevent further infection.

20

CHILDREN WITH SPECIAL NEEDS

It is very important to identify the special needs of children. It is always good to seek professional advice when you are doubtful of your child's health.

Underachievement

Children who are underachievers or developmentally delayed acquire skills at an unusually slow rate. The earliest indications may be obvious when your child shows signs of docility and quietness, and sleeps for very long periods. You may find your baby oblivious of all the noises around and not react to them. He will not interact with his environment in the same way as an average child. He may be late in smiling or learning to chew.

You will notice that as you try to engage his attention, it wanders after a few moments. Instead of concentrating all his energy on a particular task, he will spend short periods doing lots of different things. As he grows older he may tend to be overactive, and may have a lower than average I Q.

You will notice that your developmentally delayed child will take his own time in crossing the usual milestones in life.

You must make sure that he does not suffer from a physiological problem such as partial deafness. He could be suffering from a severe developmental disorder, such as dyslexia, or just be developing at a below-average rate. Your child may need remedial help.

Your baby starts becoming aware of his hands at about two months after he has begun to play with his feet. At around 12-16 weeks, your baby will stare at his hands, and turn his fist all ways, becoming enamoured with the movements. In a developmentally delayed infant, the hand observation may go on as long as five months.

Try putting your finger into a baby's palm and you observe that he grips it tightly with his fingers, a reflex action. This actions lasts for about six weeks after birth, but will last longer if your child is developmentally delayed.

Your baby will want to put everything that he can into his mouth at the age of six weeks. This behaviour will last a year in a normal child.

An infant up to the age of 16 months will start chucking objects out of his pram or crib, while a developmentally delayed child may take longer.

While dribbling normally stops at around one year of age, in developmentally delayed children, the dribbling may be present even at 18 months.

To overcome all these obstructions in learning, you must encourage your infant to interact with other people, and to use his senses from an early age. If you see that he is lagging behind, spend more time with him, talking and reading aloud to him, playing with him, showing him new things as you take him out more often. Encourage him to play more games with his toys that are educative. Give him to see colourful picture books to look at. Do not punish him for his slowness, as this may have an adverse effect on his progress.

Dyslexia

This is the inability to read properly due to a disorder of the brain, which causes the victim to confuse various letters. It is sometimes known as 'word blindness'. It is a specific neurological disorder, and not the result of poor hearing or vision, or intelligence.

A child with dyslexia has difficulty in reading, spelling and written language. He may also face problems with numbers and memory, and may be clumsy. He may have difficulties with the spoken language too besides confusion in identifying written symbols – letters and numbers. It is different from mere slowness in learning to read, and does not indicate low intelligence – some dyslexic children are above average intelligence. Dyslexia is difficult to diagnose, although special tests for children have been devised, and it may be present to some degree in one person in 20. If your partner is dyslexis then your child is 17 times more likely to suffer the disorder.

When parents become aware of the gap between their child's obvious intelligence and his level of achievement in specific areas, then it is a cause for worry, for then he has dyslexia. You may find that your child has problems perceiving letters in the correct order, or he may confuse similarly shaped letters such as b and d, and p and q. He may have poor coordination, difficulty in remembering lists of words, numbers or letters, and the order of everyday things, such as days of the week. He is unable to tell left from right and jumbles up phrases, saying 'babby's dady' instead of 'daddy's baby'. In school he will have difficulty in learning nursery rhymes and spellings. He also finds it much more difficult to balance on one leg than children who don't have dyslexia.

If your child has dyslexia, first do acknowledge that he has a problem, and don't live in the false hope that he will catch up or will learn to read eventually. Be supportive and positive, especially if he has problems at school. Engage your child with lots of educational games.

As your child is slow in learning, and maybe far behind others in his skills at school, his self-confidence will be at a low ebb. He needs a lot of assurance and support from you at home, so be patient with him; encourage him to do things that he is good at, so that he gets back his confidence, and becomes determined to do things for himself. If he finds it difficult to handle a particular task, allow him to do it slowly and tell him not to give up.

You can help him at home by playing home-learning games. Play clapping games. Give one clap for each syllable of a word, and get your child to repeat it. Tell him to say as many words as he can, beginning with a particular letter. Make him sing songs or recite rhymes that involve sequence of things, like days of a week, or months of a year. Give him a group of words, and ask him to pick the odd one out. Encourage your child to trace words or letters, or to make letters out of plasticine.

Asthma

This is a disorder of the bronchial tubes, causing difficulty in breathing. Most asthmatic attacks are mild, but the condition is a chronic one, and if it remains untreated, the consequences can be serious.

Basically, there are two major causes of asthma. The first is an infection of the nose, sinuses, bronchi (tubes leading to the lungs) or lungs, such as bronchitis. The second, and more common, type of asthma is caused by an allergic reaction that is usually inherited.

In allergic asthma, the individual may be sensitive to pollen, house dust, animal hairs, molds, insecticides, certain foods, drugs or other chemicals. When he comes in contact with them, the substance histamine is released in his system, triggering the allergic reaction. Infection and allergy can both produce asthma in the same person. In either case, the membrane lining the bronchial passage swell, narrowing the airways and making it difficult to breathe.

In a typical attack, the individual feels tightness in his chest; he wheezes, coughs, and has difficulty in breathing. His face may turn blue, and there may be a feeling of suffocation. It can be extremely frightening but is not generally dangerous. Towards the end of the acute attack, a thick mucus is coughed up and there is a feeling of relief.

Treatment consists in bringing any infection under control, generally with antibiotics. A course of injections may be prescribed to reduce sensitivity. Breathing exercises, under the supervision from a physiotherapist, may help.

To bring an asthmatic attack under control, an inhaler of isoprenaline, adrenaline or salbutamol may be used. In severe cases a doctor may inject hydrocortisone into a vein. Many children do get better as they grow older.

Your doctor will help you to chart out a management plan, explaining when to use the preventer and reliever, and what steps to take if your child's symptoms get worse. If you notice wheezing and coughing in your child early in the morning, or increased symptoms after exercise exertion, waking at night with a cough or a wheeze, or see your child using the reliever very often, you must consult your doctor.

Keep your emergency plan ready, and at hand, for any asthma attack can be life threatening. At the start of the attack, give your child his usual reliever. Wait for about 10 minutes, and if he does not get relief, send for an ambulance. Repeat the treatment until breathing improves or help arrives. If your doctor has prescribed steroid tablets, then give him one. Let your child be in an upright position till he gets into a hospital.

Cystic Fibrosis

This is a rare disease of young children in which the sweat glands and the mucus-secreting glands do not function properly, and the lungs and pancreas become involved. The child suffers from malnutrition and respiratory infections, and he loses weight. Cystic fibrosis is among the most serious lung diseases of children. It is also known as muco-viscidosis and pancreatic fibrosis. The general symptoms are decreased or poor appetite, weight loss, tummy aches, frequent or loose stools, increased or frequent cough, vomiting, increased sputum or change in its colour, breathlessness, unwillingness to exercise, fever, and common cold.

To combat the loss in weight, the patient is put on a high-protein diet, with vitamin supplements. Pancreatic extract is given to help digestion and extra salt must be taken.

Respiratory diseases are treated with antibiotics. A respiration or a plastic mist tent is used to loosen the thick mucus clogging the air passages. Physiotherapy also helps to free the lungs of mucus and to ventilate them.

Diabetes Mellitus

Diabetes mellitus, simply diabetes, is a disorder in which the body is unable to control the use of sugar as a source of energy.

Diabetes mellitus in children is largely due to insufficient insulin, and in severe cases there is no insulin at all. Glucose is not used by the body but accumulates in the blood (hyperglycaemia), and is eventually passed unused in the urine.

In severe diabetes, stored body fat releases fatty acids into the bloodstream. These are used instead of glucose as an energy source and, in turn, produce harmful substances called ketones. Without treatment, this leads to keto-acidosis, diabetic coma and death.

Skilfully make your child accept his condition, as the onset of diabetes can be swift and may take some time to stabilise. Most diabetic children need insulin injections, and a strictly controlled diet. A proper diet with restricted carbohydrate foods is essential in all forms of treatment. Its object is to give a balanced diet, meeting the nutritional needs of the patient, and at the same time keeping his weight normal.

You must teach your child to learn self-care and control. Since diabetes neglected can be dangerous the parents as well as the diabetic child tends to worry. They feel tired and confused, and they have to plan ahead when leaving home for school. They should to carry some sweets or sugar in case of emergencies, and insulin and syringe if they have to take insulin at midday. You have to be sympathetic without being over protective. You will need to help your child with his insulin injections and regularise his meals. As he grows older he will learn self-care and understand what needs to be done.

Cerebral Palsy

This is a disability, caused by damage to the developing brain, which may occur to the baby in the womb or after birth. Sometimes, the brain is formed abnormally for no apparent reason, or the disorder is inherited even if both parents are healthy. The affected area is usually one of the parts of the brain that controls the muscles and certain body movements. Normally there is interference with the messages that normally pass from the brain to the body.

Typical disabilities include poor muscular coordination, weakness and muscular spasms that interfere with movement, and speech disturbances. A child with the condition is generally known as spastic.

The degree of disability varies greatly. In mild cases, the condition may not be noticed until the child has difficulty performing acts normal for a child of his age, such as grasping objects or learning to walk. Typical signs include odd movements of the arms, legs and head, inability to coordinate movements, tremors and a stiff 'scissors' gait. In severe cases, vision, speech and hearing may be affected, and the child may have convulsions.

Many different causes can be responsible for the brain damage associated with cerebral palsy. It may be due to a rhesus haemolytic condition, insufficient oxygen before birth, premature birth, injury during birth, diseases such as encephalitis and scarlet fever, or other causes.

Approximately half of all spastic children have the intelligence of normal children. Due to their condition, however, they may sometimes appear sub-normal. The child may slobber and grimace or utter incomprehensible sounds. The fact that a child has trouble in expressing himself does not necessarily mean that he is mentally retarded.

Treatment varies with the severity and type of cerebral palsy. In severe cases, surgery may be used to some of the physical aspects of the disease. The convulsions are treated with phenobarbitone or other drugs.

Many cases are mild, and a reasonably normal life is possible. For more severe cases, a carefully developed treatment programme can lead to marked improvement. The emphasis must be put on training the child to help himself and build his self-confidence. You can help your child to use his hands right from the beginning by letting him feel things with different textures, and encouraging him to hold toys and have other objects. It will help him if you have the toys securely strung over his chair. Encourage him to learn shapes by showing him simple shaped objects, and telling him to handle and play with them. While you are busy with your everyday tasks, let him watch you, and if he likes to help, like any other normal child, let him join in if possible. With persistence and encouragement, even severe cases can make remarkable progress.

Physiotherapy, aimed especially at the development of the muscle, is important in any programme. Speech training may also be needed.

Epilepsy

This is a disorder of the nervous system in which there may be periodic loss of consciousness accompanied by convulsive seizures. The convulsions are not usually harmful. With the help of drugs, some features of the seizures can be brought under control, and in many cases they can be completely prevented.

Epilepsy is a symptom of brain damage although the condition is usually not progressive, and epileptics have a normal span of life. There appears to be a slight hereditary tendency to some types of epileptic seizures, but general medical opinion is that in most cases the hereditary factor is small.

The severest and most common type of seizure is called grand mal. It is sometimes preceded by a sensation that recurs before each attack but differs from person to person. The person with epilepsy loses consciousness and, if he is standing, falls to the ground. Convulsions follow; he thrashes about and foams at the mouth. The seizure generally lasts only a few minutes, or if one seizure immediately follows another, the condition may be more serious and a doctor should be called.

A lesser type of seizure, petit mal, is most often seen in children, who may outgrow it. The child suddenly seems to be dreaming or absent-minded. There may be slight twitching or blinking, but there is no falling or convulsion. The attack is over in a few seconds although there may be many attacks in a single day.

If your child has convulsion, there is no cause for alarm. Ideally, he should be laid on the ground away from anything on which he might injure himself. If possible, place a thick, rolled-up handkerchief between his jaws to keep him from biting his tongue or lips. But if his jaws are firmly closed, do not try to force them apart. Turn him on his side, making sure the air passage is clear in case he vomits.

Do not stop the child's medication without first seeking medical advice. Treat the child as normally as possible all the time.

Sickle Cell Anaemia

In this hereditary disorder, the red blood cells become deformed into irregular, pointed shapes resembling sickles when they are deprived of oxygen. The deformed cells do not slip easily through capillaries, and circulation is impaired. Symptoms, including severe pain in the abdomen and the joints, develops when the patient uses up much oxygen in strenuous exercise or in illnesses such as pneumonia. Sickle-cell anaemia is found among West Indians and Africans, and also occurs in some parts of India and the Mediterranean area.

When your child starts attending school, the teaching staff must be informed about his condition, making them aware of the problems it can impose on his education. Your child might have to be hospitalised, and he may miss classes. You must encourage him to express his feelings and anxieties.

There are many children who experience difficulties with their classmates. They feel alienated as their classmates think that they can catch the disease from the children with sickle cell anaemia. Your child's teacher should educate other children about this disease. There are chances that your child may think that he is the only one with this disease, or fears that he could become deformed, or die soon. Your role as a parent is to make sure that your child feels assured of your understanding, sympathy and care whenever he needs it.

21
EMOTIONAL AND PSYCHOLOGICAL PROBLEMS

All children have emotional problems that manifest in various forms like fear, anger, aggression, etc. As a parent you must ensure that your child has a conducive atmosphere for emotional stability, and a positive attitude at home. A baby too expresses its joy, anger, distress, etc., in the form of cries or a smile. By picking him up and soothing him or feeding him, calms him down; if he continues crying louder and for a longer period even after feeding, it is an indication of some distress.

When a child is happy, the glee and smile on his face tell it all. Their outlook of life, and their smiles and laughter are all indicative of a happier environment. While some children are cheerful, others may be irritable and sullen. These temperaments are inborn, but changes in their temperamental style can be effected by the way the parents handle the situation. A child who is positive-minded will adapt to changes quickly, especially the sleeping and feeding schedules. With a difficult child you may face some behavioural disorders with tantrums thrown in. If your child is slow in everything, you will need to be patient with him and give him a lot of assurances that he is doing fine, so as to boost up his self-confidence.

Fear

A child has so many things happening in his life that some of them may not be obvious to you immediately, especially something which may cause him a debilitating fear which may be fear of loud noises, like the whistle of a train, crackers bursting, the sound of thunder, etc. As he grows older, these latent fears grow with his fertile imagination and fantasies, and a lot of curiosity. He learns the dangers of certain actions and objects, and the reason why this is so. This realisation makes him very careful and sometimes frightened.

Normally parents who are over-protective of children, for whom eating or toilet training is an issue, are liable to have fears. All children have certain fears at some stage of their life, though they overcome them before their parents notice these fears. Most of these fears gradually disappear naturally as the child starts to realise that these fears have no foundation and cannot be a threat to them in any way. It is very important that the parents understand a child's fears and help him to overcome them.

Fear of the Dark

A child's inability to see clearly in the dark activates his imagination, leading him to imagine that somebody is creeping up on him. He will not enter a dark room alone, and at most times, probably the parents are to be blamed for instilling fear in them to keep them out of mischief. Sometimes a child carries this fear even into his adulthood, when he will hesitate to go alone in the dark.

The parents should be supportive in their help to the child to overcome this fear. They have to skilfully reason out and explain the situation in a realistic way, at times demonstrating by going into a dark room and showing the child that there is nothing there which can cause them undue fear. Ridiculing, punishing or scolding will only produce adverse effects. If your child is scared of the dark, keep a light lamp on in his room. Leave his door open in the night, and your voices in your bedroom floating into his room will be reassuring to him. This will subside his fears, and he will be able to step into the dark without any fear.

Tangible Fears

Sometimes, children develop fear of tangible things like water, dogs, cockroaches, etc. Normally they love to play with animals, like dogs, cats, lambs, etc., but if a strange dog snaps at them suddenly or bares its teeth, or a cat scratches them, their fear of animals commences, and grow with them unless their parents help them to get over this fear, explaining to them that not all animals behave similarly, and that they should play with those that do bark softly or purr sweetly rather than those which are strangers to them. He may soon grow out of this fear.

Children may fear water, getting into it and imagining themselves drowning in it. You can help your child by the thrill of sitting in a small basin of water and splashing in it. Gradually you introduce him to a bigger tub, then a bathtub, and gradually he can take swimming lessons, which will help him get over his small fears.

Stranger Anxiety

Your child may feel insecure when a visitor to your house picks him up, and he may cry as the visitor is a stranger to him. You can minimise this fear by placing him on your lap, facing the visitor and talking to him in a cheerful and pleasant tone. This will bring a sense of assurance to your child that the stranger is not one to be feared.

Everything has its time, so give your child time to get over his fears. He should never be ridiculed or scolded. Be compassionate and sympathise with him. Try to reassure him and help him get back his self-confidence. You can teach him some deep breathing exercises that will help him to relax the various muscles of the body in a systematic fashion, and gain control over them. So when fear of something crops up suddenly, he may find it easier to get over it sooner.

Jealousy

Sibling rivalry is very common among children. The relationship between them can be one of pleasantness, of sharing, of contentment, or can be one of rivalry, jealousy and resentment. When a baby is born in a family, the older child may feel left out and neglected, as now all the attention will be focused on the newborn. As parents, you have to handle the situation in a very skilful manner, so that your older child feels part of the family and does not resent the arrival of his sibling.

Rivalry results when two compete. You can help in minimising this rivalry by showing your love and appreciation to each child the way he is.

Before the arrival of the baby, it is essential that you prepare your first-born about his sibling's arrival. You can break the news to him about three or four months before the baby is born. You can invoke him in little things for the arrival of the baby, by asking him to help you while choosing clothes for him. Before you go into labour, let him know that you have to go to the hospital to deliver the baby while his father will be with him and take care of him.

When your child comes to you airing his grievances against his sibling, empathise with him, and acknowledge that you understand. By listening to his woes he will become calm and may soon forget his grievances. Since no two children are alike, treat them as individuals in your approach to affection, criticism, discipline and praise.

Never be partial to any one child. Treat them as equals, and teach them to share. Provide them with plenty of opportunities to play together and exchange or share toys. When the younger child gets a toy of your older child, explain to him that he cannot take it without his brother's permission, but do not pull it out of his hands or scold him. When your older child has outgrown a particular toy, let him decide when he wants to hand it down to his sibling. Be sure to praise him for the act.

A child's jealousy may be manifested in his actions. He may pinch the newborn, so don't punish him or scold him, but try to make him understand that his action has hurt the baby and that it is wrong to hurt anyone. Never leave your older child alone with the baby unless you are sure that your older child will not misbehave. Keep all sharp objects away from his reach.

You need to take some time each day to spend exclusively with your older child. Try not to make comparisons between your children. Love and encouragement will help your child to share his love with you and the baby.

Aggression

Aggression is part of the growing up process for most toddlers. Since their vocabulary is limited, they need to express their emotions, so pushing and hitting are their normal way of expressing them. They might also bite or pinch when they feel threatened. They are unable to handle a particular situation, and words fail them, so they resort to biting which gives them a lot of satisfaction of a job well done.

A child may know that pinching hurts, but he still carries out the act as he lacks control of his impulses. When he knows that he cannot control the particular situation in the way he wants to, he responds in the best way known to him, by pinching a playmate or snatching his toy, or by even biting him. He asserts himself aggressively in order to feel important. He may feel sorry when he sees his friend crying, but is helpless after the act. He might resort to an aggressive behaviour if he feels neglected, especially with the arrival of a newborn baby in the family. He may retaliate by pushing the baby or pinching him.

A toddler may resort to biting when he is hungry, bored or fatigued. This sort of tantrum may just be another sensory experiment. Biting can be just a way of expression for a child to say 'I love you', or a need for your attention and love. Biting in toddlers is something that all parents dread for it bruises and terrorises its small victims and enrages its larger ones. You may find your child biting his nails in frustration to get what he wants from another child, maybe a toy.

An aggressive instinct in a toddler cannot be overcome naturally. A child needs to get over such behaviour with your help. You need to teach him to overcome it. When he becomes aggressive, respond to it quickly. Remove him from the situation for three or four minutes, which will give him time to connect that the brief time out is a sort of punishment. For that brief period he will be missing all the fun. Each time he acts aggressively, respond to it the same time every time. Gradually he will come to realise that if he gets a time out for three or four minutes, he will be missing on all the fun.

Be always firm, but gentle, with your child when he throws tantrums. Never hit him, for he will emulate you, and start hitting others. So avoid bullying him too. Reward him for his good behaviour every time so that he will always try to be good, and not resort to violence or aggression. Keep a calendar and mark the days he has been good. At the end of the month, you can tell him how good he has been and treat him to an ice-cream or anything that he likes.

All children need to expend their energy. So channelise this energy to useful games, which are healthy and relaxing to the mind, so that they have no room for frustrations or anger. Keep him engaged so that he does not get up to any mischief.

Shyness

Shyness arises out of nervousness in a child. Basically, he is uncomfortable amidst other children, and fears rejection. This makes him nervous and stops him from saying or doing something that is expected of him. A shy child will talk less, and whenever he talks, it will be in a soft or small voice. He may not be bold enough to make eye contact, or hold his head high. He may show little facial expression, nod a lot, and keep fidgeting.

Both genetic and environmental influence may be attributed to shyness. When parents spend very little time with their child, he is likely to withdraw into himself, and may thus become very reserved and shy. A feeling of inadequacy may also result along with an inferiority complex, especially when he is amongst guests at a party. Some children are born timid, and seem to withdrawn from everything around them, even from parents, teachers and friends.

In most cases parents neglect excessive shyness as they fail to detect it. They may feel proud to be the parents of such a soft, gentle and quiet child, little realising the repercussions of such neglect. They may probably realise the gravity of the situations only when their child is unable to participate in normal social and school activities, such as playing with other children, participating in a competition or a drama, etc. He is unable to make friends, and remains a loner.

You have to build up his confidence in himself. You have to make him understand that it is not necessary to be perfect in all situations, and that he is capable of doing things like other children. Drill in him, 'I can do it' instead of 'I can't do it'. Tell him to remove the 't' from 'can't', and things will be fine. Encourage him to play with other children in your neighbourhood.

Speech Problems

There may be several reasons why someone cannot speak properly or clearly. It can be because of a physical abnormality, an emotional problem, or damage to the speech centre of the brain or the nerves to the organs of speech in the neck. Missing teeth or badly fitting dentures may make talking difficult, and malformation of the nose or tongue, or an abnormality of the larynx, may prevent the production of normal speech sounds. Harelip and cleft palate may also cause speech problems. Many of these physical causes can be corrected by dentistry or surgery.

Stuttering and stammering are two related forms of speech disorders, often of a psychological origin. Someone who stutters has difficulty in starting a sentence and repeats a sound – usually the first syllable of a word – spasmodically; someone who stammers involuntarily repeats a syllable, or even a whole word. The two terms are often used interchangeably.

A person who stammers will experience hesitancies and silent pauses, with tensions in his jaws or cheeks, and blinking repeatedly. He may be reluctant to introduce himself, answer phones, participate in debates or talk in school.

When a person lisps, the letters 's' and 'z' are pronounced like 'th', for example, 'thoo' for 'zoo' or 'tharing' for 'sharing'. This is because the jaw or teeth are malformed. If a child lisps and his or her mouth is normal, speech training can cure it. Place a straw in your child's drink, for that makes him use his lips, and the sucking action develops good oral strength, which is important for speech correction. Blowing bubbles is a good option, as also blowing into a horn, for the effort needed to make a solid sound strengthens the muscles of the cheeks, and tends to push the tongue back in. A child with a cold or allergies should be attended to and treated immediately as a stuffy nose always hampers speech.

When a child stutters, you may notice tension in his jaws or cheeks, as he is trying in his excitement or anger to get the words out at once. He may blink repeatedly also. When you see such symptoms consult your doctor at once. It is very important for you, as parents, to know how to respond to your child who stutters. Be sure to keep your voice soft and speech slow so that he will follow your lead. Be patient with him, have eye contact and smile to give him a lot of assurance and love.

Stuttering is often caused by an emotional shock, or it may be a family trait. It usually starts in childhood, although sometimes it does not occur until adolescence. Someone who stutters is often left-handed.

In many cases speech therapy produces good results. This may include training in breath control, together with psychological treatment to remove any emotional disorder. A childhood stammer may be psychological, and some experts maintain that it is caused by deep-seated conflicts affecting the speech centre in the brain.

A deaf child needs special speech training because he cannot hear other people's voices – or his own – in order to know what sounds are like.

If a stammer develops later in life the cause is definitely psychological, and if the underlying cause of anxiety is removed, the stammer disappears.

However, if a speech disorder is caused by damage to the speech centre of the brain, it is impossible to cure it.

What you can do to help your child is not to be correcting him all the time that will make him very conscious.

Always maintain eye contact with your child, and use meal time as conversation time. By talking slowly to him, he will learn to imitate you and do the same. If he stammers, be patient and smile, so that he feels assured, and carries on with his conversation. A calm and pleasant atmosphere at home will help him to have a relaxed frame of mind, and help him to get over his speech problem.

22
BEHAVIOURAL PROBLEMS AT SCHOOL

Many children have behavioural problems at school, like problems with homework, problems related to bullying and teasing, and school avoidance.

Homework Problem

One of the first responsibilities that a child has is doing his homework. It involves not only the child in learning and being responsible for completing it, but also the parents in motivating and supporting the efforts of the child.

Your child may neglect his homework, just because he is more interested in playing, or because he has forgotten that he had to finish what was given in class. He might not like writing work, and may devise ways to escape from doing his homework.

You must encourage your child to think, assess and respond on his own. You must supervise his homework, but never ever do his assignment yourself. If he has problems with his homework do explain how he should do it, and then let him work independently. If he is unable to find an answer to a certain poser, give him a clue and elicit the answer from him for this will give him a lot of confidence and assurance that he can do it on his own merit. Ensure that he completes all the assignments that have been given in class to be completed at home.

It is very important for a child to have regular study hours, so that a discipline is set early in his life. Give him a good table and chair for himself, where he can sit and complete his homework. The table should be of the right height so that it is not a strain on his eyes or hands. Give him ample room to spread out his work, and remove all unnecessary clutter from the table. See that noises from outside, or from a television or radio do not distract him. Provide him with a good supply of stationery so that he does not make lack of it as an excuse to skip doing his homework. Also make sure that you do not have a phone connection nearby.

Bullying and Teasing

Many parents receive complaints from school about their child's misbehaviour. This could be many, but whatever they are, you need to correct this behaviour in your child before it is too late.

Sometimes, the child bullies others for he himself has been a victim of bullying. He may have a very low esteem of himself, and to get over this complex, he bullies others to show that he is powerful, or in control. He may also use this tactic if he feels that he will become popular among his friends by doing so.

There are various types of bullying, some of which are hitting, pushing and shoving, biting, punching, etc., which are physical forms. Then a verbal form would be calling names, persistent teasing or spreading rumours. Emotional bullying involves excluding a child from group activities, and hampering him emotionally.

When you notice that your child has bruises on his body, or he refuses to go to school, you must find out the reasons. It could probably be that someone who considers him a soft target for bullying is bullying him at school. Your child may suddenly have a mysterious illness or stomach ache when it is time to set out to school, or he may suddenly be reluctant to go out and play with his friends. These are indications that he is feeling low and insecure, probably because he does not know how to handle the situation of being bullied.

A child can be an easy target for bullying if he is more anxious and insecure than his peers. He may be very intelligent and score good marks, which gives room for jealousy to his peers and an excuse to bully him. If they realise that the child is weak natured and docile, then they make him a scapegoat for their bullies.

As parents, you must talk with your child and try to find out why he gives in to being bullied. Assure him that you understand him, and comfort him that you are always there for him to share his problems with. Never over-react as this can have an adverse effect on his progress. Explain to him that children who are unhappy or insecure bully others. Give a lot of assurance to your child, and help him to stand up for him, be bold and courageous, look into the bully's eyes and say boldly, "I do not like your teasing, so stop it at once!" Tell him to remain with a big group, as there will be less chances of his being bullied.

Do not get angry if you realise your child is a bully, but talk to him and find out what is troubling him, for bullying is a sign of insecurity. Spend a lot of time with him, and pay attention to his needs. Have a good rapport with him, and get him to share all the day's happenings with you. Explain to his teacher that he is changing for the better, so that the teacher too can cooperate and help the child get over his bullying ways.

School Avoidance

Children carry strong feelings as toddlers to their school-going age, and later as adults, and school may trigger off an old feeling that they are not welcome. They resist change, and the first change may be being away from their parents when they go to school. It may not be that a child does not going to school so much as that he will be away from the secure fold of his home and parents. Having all these days been cocooned in safety and love at home, he may find the daily transition from home to school difficult.

Another cause could be the fear of school itself. Parents are heard to say, "If you do not finish your food I will tell your teacher to punish you." This creates an impression in him that a teacher is someone who is to be feared.

You can help your child to look forward to going to school everyday. When he sets out of the house towards school, give him warm hugs and have some friendly chat with him, so that he goes off in a cheerful mood. Do not hurry him out of the house, but talk him to something pleasant, like about a friend whom he likes, or about his favourite snack that you have packed for him for snack time at school. By being supportive, you can help him to build up his confidence. Never show your impatience or bad moods as he leaves for school as this may affect his mood also.

You can usually size up your child's unhappiness at school by a few tell-tale indications. If you notice a recurring problem of stomach pains or diarrhoea before going to school, it may be because he is worried or scared about someone or something at school. You may notice that he suddenly starts biting his nails, sucking his thumb, or wetting his bed. He withdraws into his shell or goes very quiet when you mention his school or teacher. He might suddenly be rebellious and refuse to go to school. These may be indications that something or someone is worrying him.

There are certain ways in finding out how your child feels about school. Volunteer to help in his class, and you will get to see how he interacts with others kids, what is bugging him, how he relates with his teachers, how he responds to questions posed by his teacher, etc.

It is also vital that you have a good rapport with your child so that he can confide in you all the nagging worries that are bothering him. You should get in touch with his teacher to find out more about what is bothering him in school.

It is important for the child to know that you have good communications with his teacher, so that there is regular flow of information both ways. So get to know his teacher right from the beginning, and keep in touch with her/him. Don't forget to thank his teacher when she shows special sensitivity towards your child. Take action if a problem arises, but be discreet. If you are angry with the teacher, do not criticise her in front of your child.

23

INCULCATING GOOD HABITS IN CHILDREN

It is very important for children to be taught the importance of good manners, sharing, good habits and responsibilities from a very early age. A self-confident child can handle simple situations easily, and learns to face them with grace and dignity.

Politeness is something that a child picks up from his parents and others who influence his life. If you have your parents or grandpatents with you, your child emulates the way you treat them. This is where parents can mould a child's character, and imbibe in him the essentials of good habits and manners.

Babies are too young to learn habits or manners. By about one year, when they are picking up words, they can be taught words like 'please', 'thank you' and 'sorry'. As you speak to the child, he can see these words spilling from your lips, and they are at an impressionable age when they imitate you and pick up these words. This will be a solid foundation of imbibing good manners and habits.

As your infant grows older and mixes with other children, he should be disciplined to say 'thank you' and 'please', and be polite with grown-ups, with his friends, his teachers, etc. You may have to keep reminding him of his manners, since children do have a short memory.

Set good examples yourself. When he gives you something, say 'thank you' to him, or if by accident you bang against him, tell 'sorry'. These little gestures leave an imprint in his mind, and he will soon be repeating them himself.

Teach your child how to greet someone and how to bid them goodbye. If you do so every time you have visitors and they leave, then your child is bound to pick up these simple courtesies.

Teach him the blessing of sharing. Buy a bar of chocolate, cut it into pieces, put them on a plate, and ask him to hand it around. Similarly, buy two toys of similar shape, colour and size, and ask him to give one to his neighbour friend.

It is very difficult to teach a child to be patient, but you can make a beginning. Ask him to fall in line behind a queue of boys or girls, and wait for his chance to hand over the birthday gift, or fill up his plate, or have a go at the swing. Teach him how to greet someone, and not wait for the other person to greet him first. And if he hurts someone either accidentally or intentionally, he must not hesitate to go up to the person and apologise, saying 'sorry'.

Teach him etiquette at the dining table. He must learn to eat without spilling too much, and not talk too much. Teach your child to thank God for the food that he is about to eat. See that he learns to sit straight in his chair and does not slouch. If he does not want to eat something, he must be taught how to refuse it politely.

By the age of ten they would have picked up some good habits. If they attend the phone, teach them basic manners, like, "Many I know who is speaking, please?" Or "Please hold on, I shall fetch him." If guests come, he must greet them, and if they have children, he can share his toys with them.

When children are born, they do not have the sharing instinct innate in them. They are too young to see things from another's perspective, but as he matures, he learns to share things at his own pace.

For a child, the first instinct is to have possession of something, say, a toy. He may take pleasure in showing it to someone but will not give it away or lend it. As he grows older he begins by sharing simple things like a biscuit or a chocolate, but not a toy, which he values very much. He may one day give it away of his own accord, but never force him to do so. Your child may like a toy that another child possesses, and may try to grab it. Do not scold him, but try to explain to him that the toy does not belong to him, and that he has better toys at home.

Children have no concept of borrowing or lending. Once something is given to someone on loan, he feels it has gone away for good, and that he will not get it lack. They would rather share than lend. Make sharing fun for your kid. Involve him in a group game where everyone joins in to complete a work, like a jigsaw puzzle.

Never tell your child that he is selfish, for he might become resentful and rebellious. Give him a lot of assurance to make him feel secure, for insecurity creates problems in sharing. Teach him to respect the possessions of other children, and if he does handle them, then to do it with care. It is quite likely that he may not wish to share his toys with a particular kid who is destructive. If such a situation arises, put away the toys, and teach your child not to play with them in the presence of the other kid. After all, you do not wish to hurt the sentiments of the other child.

When you see your child voluntarily sharing his things with others, give him a word of praise, and commend his actions. This in itself will be justifiable reward.

Teach your child to be responsible for his things. It will take time for him to be disciplined, but be patient with him, and set good examples so that he learns to follow them.

At the toddler stage, your child will not know the value of responsibility, but you can start with little things. For example, when he picks up a toy from the toy box, show him how he has to put it back where it belongs, after he has finished playing with it. If you see it lying around, take him gently by the hand, pick up the toy, give it to him, and take him to the toy box, telling him to put it inside. As he grows older, teach him other simple things, like putting soiled clothes in a basket, school shoes on the shoe rack, schoolbag on his writing table, etc. By the age of seven he should be able to make his bed when he wakes up.

At every step of a child's life, set an example, so that the child would also want to do it. He may help you in making the bed; he may want to help you in the kitchen in his own way. Give him small things to do if he is interested, like stringing beans, laying the table, wiping the plates, etc.

A school-going child should know that he is responsible for his books, stationery, etc. He must be responsible for his homework, and may seek help. If he has a separate room, teach him how to keep it tidy. The day it is very neat, don't fail to praise him. This will be a great incentive for him to earn more praises from you and friends, and hence will always strive for cleanliness. Help him to become a positive child.

24

FIRST AID AND IMMUNISATION

As a parent, you will have to cope with common minor injuries that happen in and around the home, like cuts, bruise and burn, as your child grows up. But you should also be prepared and equipped to cope with major accidents or emergencies, should they occur. You should know the basic first aid techniques to deal with accidents immediately, effectively and calmly. You should have a handy first aid kit in your home, away from your child's reach.

Minor injuries can be treated at home. Soil or dirt in a wound can be a source of infection, so all bruises and cuts should be washed thoroughly with soap and water, dried, and then covered with a sterile dressing. If dirt is embedded in a cut or scratch, consult a doctor, or take the child to hospital in case an antibiotic or anti-tetanus injection is necessary.

Bites

Insect bites can generally be relieved with calamine lotion or anti-histamine cream. If complications develop, consult a doctor.

Animal bites usually respond to cleaning with soap and water, and an antiseptic dressing. A dog-bite may need to be treated with an anti-rabies injection. Let a doctor see it at the first opportunity in case there are any complications with an animal bite. Animal bites are seldom serious, and soon heals if there is no infection.

Bites by gnats and mosquitoes cause inflammation and itching, but see that your child does not scratch the bite, as it can damage the skin. Apply calamine lotion or antihistamine cream. If complications develop within a few days of the mosquito bite, seek a doctor's advice.

For snakebite, wash the wound with soap and water, and apply a dry dressing on it. Rest the child, and see that he does not move the bitten part. Do not give him anything to drink or eat. Arrange for him to be taken on a stretcher in an ambulance to hospital. If he shivers, feels sick or complains of giddiness after 15 minutes, then the poison has got into the system. He has to be hospitalised and be under the care of a doctor till the venom has been eliminated from his body.

Bleeding

Minor bleeding usually stops on its own or under slight pressure. If there is dirt in or around the wound, wash with soap and water, and dry with cotton swabs, wiping away from the wound.

Minor bleeding usually stops of its own accord, but can be controlled by pressure from a pad or dressing, or even bare fingers.

If the bleeding is severe, make the victim lie still while an ambulance is called for. If the wound is in an arm or leg and no facture is suspected raise the limb above the level of the rest of the body. Apply dry dressings to the wound. If they become soaked with blood, do not remove them but press more on top.

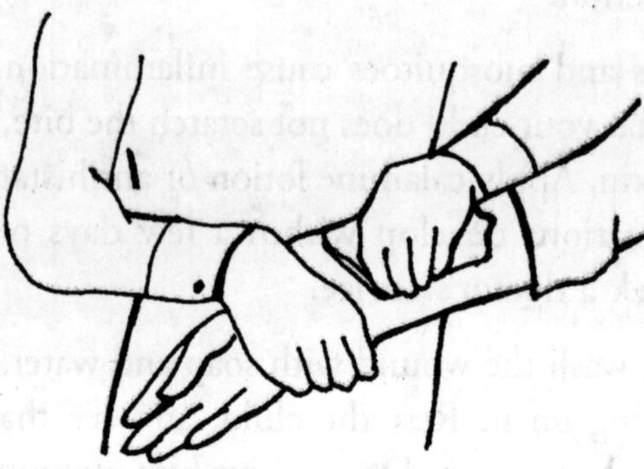

Press a dressing on the wound

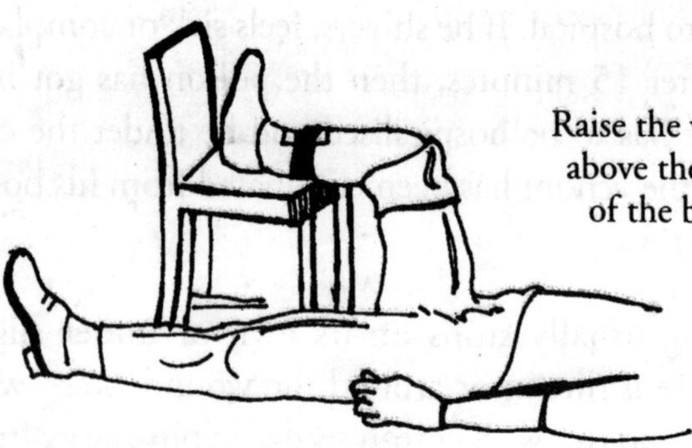

Raise the wound above the level of the body

If there is internal bleeding, it may be revealed by paleness, breathlessness or restlessness. Blood may be coughed up, vomited or passed in the stools or urine. Only a doctor can treat internal bleeding.

Bleeding in the tissues causes bruises such as that which sometimes accompanies a closed fracture.

If the victim is vomiting, lay him in the recovery position on his stomach with his head turned to one side and the arm and leg of that side drawn up; otherwise lay him in as comfortable a position as possible. Loosen all clothing and get him to hospital as quickly as possible, preferably by ambulance, which will not jolt him, unlike other forms of transport.

If there is nose bleeding in your child, make him sit with his head forward and over a bowl. Pinch his nostrils together firmly for up to ten minutes. By that time the bleeding should stop. If it does not, pinch the nostrils again for another five minutes. If that does not stop the bleeding get your child to hospital. If he loses a lot of blood, consult a doctor.

Bruises

Internal bleeding from tiny blood vessels in the tissues causes these. Cold wet compresses, such as ice packs or clean cloths wrung out under cold water, reduce swelling. Rest allows the blood to clot and helps to stop bleeding. If a large and painful swelling develops from a bruise, consult a doctor.

Burns and Scalds

Only shallow burns or scalds should be treated at home; others should be referred to a doctor.

For a minor burn or scald, put the affected part under cold running water until the pain has stopped, then cover it with a sterile dressing. Do not put oil or a greasy ointment on it – it causes pain when it has to be removed.

Do not apply cotton wool or any fluffy dressing. Do not apply soap, and do not burst any blisters. Do not give your child anything to drink unless there is likely to be a delay of more than 30 minutes before medical help arrives. If such a delay is likely, give him about half a cup of water if he wants to drink.

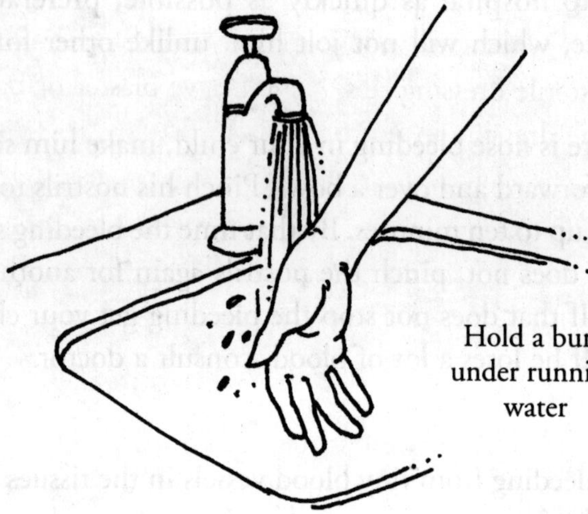

Hold a burn under running water

Choking

An object sticking in the throat is a usual cause. The obstruction can often be loosened and removed by placing your child face downwards on a bed or table, with his head and chest hanging down over the side, and thumping him between the shoulder blades. A young child or baby should be help upside-down and his back slapped.

The objective in a choking situation should be to dislodge the object that is blocking the throat and preventing normal breathing.

Your child may be coughing violently. If the coughing does not clear the blockage, give him a hard slap between the shoulder blades. Do not try to remove the object with your fingers; you are likely to push it further down the throat. If first aid does relieve choking, take your child immediately to a hospital, and remember that time is all-important.

Cuts

Thoroughly wash a minor cut with soap and water, and cover it with a sterile dressing. Use an adhesive plaster or bandage to hold the dressing in position.

A small cut should heal quickly and leave little or no scar; but if pus and inflammation form, consult a doctor.

Remember that even a deep puncture leaves only a small cut on the surface, but the internal damage may be more serious and can carry infection into the tissues.

A deep cut may need stitching: consult a doctor or a hospital if there is any doubt. And consult a doctor if the bleeding is extensive or persistent.

Eye Injury

To dislodge a piece of dirt or dust from the eye, ask your child to blink rapidly a few times: the movement itself may dislodge the dirt or may cause an increase in the tear flow, which could also remove the object.

If that fails, pull the upper eyelid over the lower one, then release it. If the foreign body is still in the eye and is causing pain, and it can be seen on the white of the eye or on the underneath of the upper eyelid, try to remove it with the corner of a clean handkerchief.

Do not persist if a visible object in the eye cannot be wiped away; it is probably embedded and needs treatment by a doctor.

Fainting

If a child faints, loosen all tight clothing round his neck, chest and waist, lay him on one side and draw up the arm and leg of the uppermost side. If he feels faint, get him to lie down or sit with his head between his knees.

Put your head between your knees if you feel faint

Fainting is caused by a temporary failure of the blood supply to the brain. The child has a feeling of unsteadiness, and if this is not treated he is likely to turn pale and pass out.

Fainting can be due to over-excitement, a particularly frightening event, description, sight or sound, or extreme pain. When your child faints inside the house, be sure to open the windows to improve ventilation.

Grazes

Remove gravel or splinters, preferably with tweezers that have been sterilised by immersing them in boiling water for five minutes.

Wash the wound thoroughly with soap and water, and cover it with a sterile dressing. Change the dressing daily until the wound heals.

Scratches

Jagged wounds, possibly with torn skin, are usually difficult to get clean. A small scratch or laceration stops bleeding if held under cold running water for a few minutes. Wash it with soap and water, and then cover it with a sterile dressing.

A deep laceration may need stitching; consult a doctor or take your child to the hospital.

Splinters

Wash the skin around the splinter with soap and water. Sterilise a pair of tweezers by boiling them in water for five minutes; use them to pull out the splinter. Use a magnifying glass, if necessary.

A deeply embedded splinter, or one that causes severe inflammation marked by acute pain, redness and swelling, should be extracted by a doctor.

Sprain

This arises when ligaments are overstretched or torn after a joint has been bent or twisted beyond its normal range of movement.

When an ankle is sprained, the joint and the foot swell. Remove the shoe immediately, cutting any laces to save time during which the swelling could rise and make removal of the shoe painful and difficult.

Apply ice or a cold wet cloth to the sprain, or immerse it in cold water. Rest the sprained joint in the position most comfortable for the child. In the case of an ankle, this may be by supporting the whole leg from heel to thigh; but do not let the knee bridge the gap between the seat and whatever is supporting the heel.

If necessary, put a long splint or piece of wood underneath the leg, with a thick layer of cotton around the affected, joint, and gently bandage the leg to the splint. The leg, on its splint, can then be supported on another chair without causing additional pain.

Painful joint injuries, especially where there is swelling, are usually x-rayed at a hospital to check whether any bones are broken or any ligaments are badly torn.

Stings

Insect stings are rarely more than a nuisance, and the pain and irritation usually go away within a few hours.

Remove the wound with antihistamine cream. If a bee, wasp or hornet stings, the antihistamine cream will relieve the pain. If the sting is still in the skin, first take it out with a pair of tweezers or clean fingernails. With these fairly common stings, venom is injected into the skin, which causes inflammation and local pain. In rare cases, venom can spread through the body: it then requires urgent medical treatment.

Application of antihistamine cream counteracts the extra flow in the tissues of histamine, the shock-producing substance caused by the venom injected by an insect.

If your child is stung by a nettle, relieve irritation with cream, calamine lotion or a clear cloth wrung out under cold running water. Nettle stings are uncomfortable rather than dangerous and last only a few hours.

Shock

Any child who has a serious injury or burn should be watched for signs of delayed shock, which may not develop until several hours after the injury. If signs of shock appear – weakness, extreme pallor, cold and moist skin, weak and rapid pulse, irregular and shallow breathing, thirst, nausea, scanty secretion of urine and low blood pressure – keep the child warm and call a doctor at once. Otherwise, take him to the nearest hospital. Shock due to electrocution or severe bleeding may develop suddenly and become rapidly worse, unless preventive measures are taken without delay. Always make sure that he child is lying down, and not standing.

Hiccup (Hiccough)

Ordinarily, hiccups last only a few minutes and are no cause for concern. However, if an attack is prolonged and severe do not wait until it has caused exhaustion and anxiety; consult a doctor who may prescribe a sedative.

Hiccups can be caused be eating or drinking too quickly, by disorders of the digestive tract and respiratory system, and by nervous tension.

For hiccups, that are normally mild, take a serious of deep breaths; pull the tongue, to induce swallowing; induce sneezing with pepper; drink a glass of water slowly or from the far side of the glass; and breath into a paper bag held closely about the face for no longer than a minute or two. The use of a paper bag increases the carbon dioxide content of the air breathed in so that the lungs work harder in order to get more oxygen. Often this deeper breathing regulates the contractions of the diaphragm.

Sunstroke

This is a serious upset of the body's cooling system, caused by excessive exposure to the sun or to very hot air in places having poor ventilation. The early symptoms are headache, weakness and dizziness, with a high fever (106^0 F). The skin is hot and dry, and there is no perspiration. In severe cases there may be violent vomiting, convulsions and a coma. Call a doctor promptly or get the child to a hospital. The doctor may prescribe ice bags, cold baths and other methods to bring down the temperature. He may need to give intravenous injections of fluids containing salt and sedatives if convulsions occur. After the temperature is brought down, the child should have complete rest by spending several days in bed. Give him cold drinks like cold coconut water, fresh fruit juice, etc.

Sunburn

A certain amount of exposure to the sun is necessary for the formation of vitamin D in the body. But damage to the skin by over-exposure to the sun's radiation may even cause a second-degree burn. In severe sunburn, the skin becomes covered with large, watery blisters, and is extremely painful when touched. The danger of infection of the blisters is always present. If the burn is over a large part of the body, the child may become feverish and go into shock.

While the burn is still sensitive, your child should stay out of the sun. Compresses dipped in cool water or liquid paraffin help to relieve the pain. Mild creams, such as unscented cold cream, help to restore oil and moisture to the skin.

When the skin starts to heal, the burnt layer sloughs off and may leave scars or unsightly patches. Constant tanning dries the skin and causes wrinkles; in tropical climates, it may even result in skin cancers. Various tanning lotions and creams may help to prevent sunburn. In hot weather, if your child wants to play outside, see that he wears his cap, and plays in the shade of trees.

Blisters

A blister is a collection of fluid under the skin. The fluid is usually colourless, watery serum derived from the blood. Rubbing or burning often causes it.

The fluid in a small blister is usually absorbed fairly rapidly into the tissues below it. New skin forms under the blister and, when healing is complete, the damaged skin comes off. If the epidermis, or outer layer of skin, covering a blister is removed before healing takes place underneath, it leaves a painful, moist surface of dermis (the lower layer of skin) exposed to possible invasion by infection.

Blisters on the feet, caused by a shoe rubbing against the skin, are especially prone to be rubbed open accidentally. Put a gauze dressing or adhesive plaster over a blister if it is in danger of being damaged before it heals. Do not interfere with it in any other way.

If any blister shows signs of infection, such as severe pain, inflammation or the formation of pus, take your child to your doctor.

Toothache

The most frequent cause of toothache is decay, which has penetrated the enamel and the dentine, the two outer layers of the tooth. Other causes may be an abscess, or abnormal pressure from an incorrect bite.

Toothache may be temporarily relieved by taking a mild painkiller such as aspirin, by painting the affected tooth with oil of cloves, or by placing a cloth-covered hot-water bottle on the side of the face. But for permanent relief, a dentist must treat the tooth.

Poisoning

Do not attempt to clear the poison out of the child's system. Instead call a doctor at once. If your child has stopped breathing, give him the kiss of life. Use the mouth-to-nose method if you think that there is still poison in his mouth.

If your child is unconscious but breathing, or seems likely to vomit, place him on his stomach, turn his head to one side and draw up the arm and leg of that side. Keep him in that position while waiting for medical help.

If he is conscious, ask him what poison he swallowed – he may soon lose consciousness, and the information may help the doctor in his treatment. Look for bottles, tablets, smell of petrol or kerosene; it could help the doctor to make a quick diagnosis.

Keep your child warm, and do not leave him before the doctor arrives; he may have a relapse or may stop breathing, and need further first aid.

Resuscitation

Anyone whose breathing has stopped needs artificial respiration at once. Lack of oxygen can cause brain damage within only three to five minutes, and longer oxygen starvation leads to death.

Breathing can stop from one of many reasons: drowning, electric shock, poisoning, suffocation or a sudden illness such as a heart attack.

To check whether your child is breathing put your ear close to his nose and mouth: you should be able to hear air passing in and out of his throat. Or put a mirror close to his lips: if he is breathing, the mirror mists over.

If your child stops breathing, you must carry out a few essential checks. Look in the mouth and check for obstructions, clear the airway if you can by tilting your child's head back. If he shows no signs of breathing, you will have to give him artificial ventilation, also known as the kiss of life. Check that he has a pulse. If there is none or if it is very weak, you will have to give chest compressions and the kiss of life.

The easiest way of giving artificial respiration is by blowing into the child's lungs through his mouth, his nose or the nose and mouth together for a very small child or boy. You should blow only hard enough to inflate the child's chest.

If the kiss of life is being applied to the mouth, the child's nostrils must be kept closed by pinching them together. If it is through the nose, the mouth must be kept closed by pushing the chin up and holding the lips together. The air blown from your lungs into the child's is good enough to re-start breathing, and to oxygenate the blood and prevent brain damage.

The child's chest should rise after air has passed into the lungs, and it should fall when the air is breathed out. If there is no movement, it is most likely that the air passage is still blocked.

Open his mouth and make sure that there is no obstruction in his throat. Check the position of the head – pull it back as far as it will go, push the chin up and blow again into child's mouth or nose.

When the child can breathe again lay him on one side, with the uppermost arm and leg drawn up. Summon medical help, if you have not already done so.

Watch his breathing if it stops again, turn him on his back and continue treatment with the kiss of life.

If you find no pulse in your child, give chest compressions with the kiss of life. Place your child on his back on a firm surface. Place the middle finger of one hand on the tip of the breastbone, and the index finger above it. Put the heel of your other hand so that it rests just above the index finger. Remove your fingers away from the breastbone, and with the heel of the other hand, press down sharply to a depth of about 3 cm. Give five compressions in three seconds. Then give artificial ventilation. Keep checking your child's pulse till he shows signs of reviving. Alternate five compressions in three seconds with one breath of ventilation. After a minute, call an ambulance, and then continue.

Home Medical Kit

Every home should have a kit of bandages and dressings in case of emergencies or for treating minor injuries. All the items should be kept out of the reach of children. A wall-mounted cupboard or an airtight box is ideal. Many people find that, in addition to the basic kit, they accumulate various other items. They may add a roll of tubular bandage for dressing fingers, special dressings for minor burns, a magnifying glass for seeing splinters, and a torch.

Bandages

Triangular bandage

Open-weave bandage

Crepe bandage

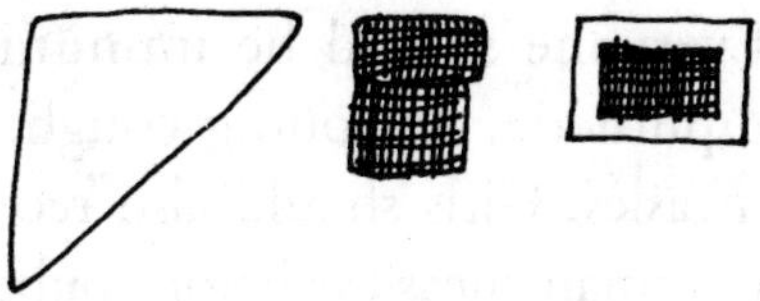

Dressings

Gauze dressings

Gauze pads

Cotton wool

Cleansing tissues

Wound dressings

Adhesive plasters

Surgical tape

Fixings

Safety pins

Bandage clips

Tweezers

Dressing scissors

Eye bath

Thermometer

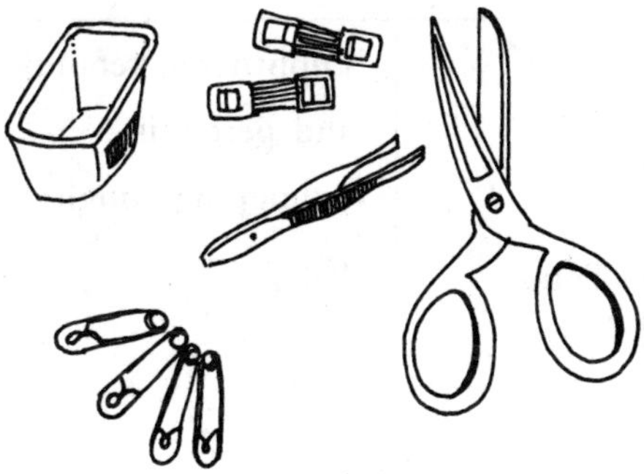

Medicines

Soluble aspirin

Indigestion tablets

Antiseptic cream

Dettol

Calamine lotion

Antihistamine cream

Liquid paracetamol

Immunisation

Everyone should be immunised at an early age against diphtheria, whooping cough, tetanus, polio myclitis and measles. Girls should also receive injections against rubella (German measles) before puberty.

Smallpox vaccination should be given to children before they are six months old. Immunity against typhoid, cholera, liphtheria, influenza, measles, mumps, poliomyelitis, rubella, sleeping sickness, tetanus, tuberculosis, whooping cough and yellow fever is necessary; hence immunisation details should be verified from health centres, and precautionary measures should be taken to safeguard your child's health.

Immunisation Programme

Injection	*Protects Against*	*Comments*
DTP	Diphtheria, tetanus and pertussis (whooping cough)	Given between 2nd and 4th month of birth.
Polio	Polio	Given by mouth between 2nd and 4th month of birth. A booster shot at the age of 5 years.
MMR	Measles, mumps and rubella	Given at 13 months or after this.

25

ASTROLOGICAL GUIDE FOR YOUR CHILD

Astrology provides the information about the future of your child. Here we are providing the information on the basis of date of birth.

ARIES CHILD (March 21 to April 20)

Aries is one of the most positive, forthright, dynamic signs of the Zodiac, so your child will always be active, both mentally and physically. Because he or she will be strong willed and determined to have his or her own way at all times, the parents will need to know how to exercise some tactful but firm discipline, otherwise this child will soon be running the household.

Mars (the mythological god of war) rules this star sign, so don't expect your child to be peace loving, meek and mild. There is a forceful, aggressive quality about Mars, so in some ways Aries is better suited to the masculine nature rather than the femininc one. If your baby is a girl, don't be surprised if she is not interested in many of the things which appeal to most little girls. She is also likely to go through a tomboy stage as she grows up.

This star sign gives an abundance of vitality, enthusiasm and stamina. You have a real bundle of energy on your hands which must find an outlet in all sorts of exciting activities, Aries is at its best when faced with a challenge, an adventure or even an opponet, but there is usually intense dislike of anything slow, dreary, repetitive or monotonous.

Parents should be alert to the fact that many Aries children are attracted to and fascinated by danger, so it is essential that they be carefully educated in all aspect of safety.

There is a natural enthusiasm for starting new interests. Activities and projects and having new things to play with but once have done so the novelty soon wears of and they quickly lose interest.

Your child has a natural inclination to rule the roost so her or she will often be bossy towards other children. When opposed or thwarted, the Aries impatience and hot temper will quickly come to the surface.

TAURUS CHILD (April 21 to May 21)

Because Taurus is the most "earthy" of all the signs, your child has a very stable nature and a contented disposition unless subjected to constant changes. These are so undesirable for this star sign because they will produce feeling of instability and insecurity.

In general, a Taurean child is a plodder (but a determined one), who does most things in life slowly but surely and according to the rules.

Venus (the mythological goddess of love and beauty) rules Taurus so these factor together with peace, tranquility, harmony and affection, will be very important to this child.

As parents you will realise early that you have a very strong willed, stubborn child on your hands whose determination "to dig the heels in" is so inflexible that he or she will often overcome your resistance. Once he or she realises you will give in you will find it difficult to reverse the situation. Start off as your wish to continue.

These children have a natural artistic sense, whether it is for beauty, design, colour, music, art or nature, so when buying books, playthings or clothes for your child be sure that they are attractive, appealing and offer a means of artistic or creative self- expression.

Taurus places great importance on feeling settled and secure. One of the ways of achieveing this is to fulfil the strong desire to own and possess things. Therefore, this child will be very reluctant to part with any of the little toys or other possessions which are treasured so much. He or she will also be quite possessive of special childhood friends and this characteristic will continue on into adulthood.

In true Taurean style this chid will learn to appreciate the value of money and even when quite young will derive much satisfaction from having a personal bank account.

GEMINI CHILD (May 22 to June 21)

Gemini is related to the mind and all mental faculties , so in general a child born under this star sign will have above average intelligence with a quick, alert, enquiring mind. However, the duality of Gemini (symbolised by the twins) gives a love of variety and change. It also confers a high degree of versatility, so there is the tendency to fit from one interest to another and unless the child learns to concentrate on one thing at a time, this superficial knowledge of many things can lead to him or her becomming a Jack of all trades and master of none.

Mercury (the winged messenger of the gods in ancient mythology) is the planet which rules Gemini, so you will find that "communication" in all its forms such as reading, writing, talking, travelling and making contact with others will always be a vital factor in this child's life. For this reason parents should give the child plenty of books, magazines, pens, pencils, paper, a toy telephone, even a toy typewriter.

Manual dexterity comes naturally, so they love do all sort of things with their hands such as fixing or making things and taking them apart to see how they work.

Gemini children are usually more restless than other star signs and since their nervous systems are highly strung they need regular periods of peace, quite and relaxation in order to give their whole system a chance to unwind. At times, your child will be a walking question mark, always asking how, when where, why and chattering on incessantly about all sorts of things. Remember that your child is very intelligent, so avoid too much "baby talk."

Gemini children naturally share their thoughts, friendship and affection with just about everyone they know because they have an innate need to mix with other people.

CANCER CHILD (June 22 to July 22)

The Moon, Cancer's ruling sphere, is intimately related to feelings and all that is gently, homely, sensitie, responsive, familiar and protective. It is essential for the parents of a Cancerian child to realise that this little person realy does need to know that he or she loved and wanted. To your moonchild, Mum, Dad, the family circle and the safe, familiar home environemt are of paramount importance, so never do anything to make a Cancerian child feel cut off, shut out, rejected or unloved. Constant reassurance will be necessary, especially during the early stages of any big changes or new cycles such as moving house or starting school because these can be traumatic experiences for such a sensitive nature.

Cancerians are very loyal, diligent, resilient and resolute. In fact, they can surprise many people because their strength of purpose is not always obvious somewhat like the iron fist in a velvet glove.

This is one of the most emotional of all the Zodiac signs and being so hypersensitive their feelings are vey easily hurt. Even a slight rebuke or a critical remark made by a friend, teacher or parent will upset the gentle Cancerian, who then proceeds to magnify it out of all proportion and worries himself or herself sick about it. There is no one who is more expert at making mountains out of molehills and when this happens the child will either cry, sink into a mood of gloom, sulk or wallow in selfpity. When parents play any type of mental or physical games with this child, let the child win because this will help to boost his or her self confidence and allay the fear of insecurity which so often plagues this particular star sign.

The material (and paternal) in stinct is very strong, so give these children something to care for such as a pet, a doll, a favourite plant.

LEO CHILD (July 23 to August 23)

The Sun, which has control over the entire solar system, is the ruler of Leo. This explains why so many people born in this star sign are natural leaders in their particular field. This basic characteristic is evident even in the very early years, so little Leos like to be big bosses taking control of other children and childhood situations. Although this air of authority and power is appropriate in certain situations it can become a real problem if the child is allowed to become a bully with an overblown sense of self importance.

Your child is warm hearted, outgoing, fun loving, with plenty of self confidence, but he or she does need to be noticed, apprreciated, praised and loved. When this is not forthcoming your child will start showing off and doing all sorts of naughty things in order to attract attention. After all, no one likes to be in the limelight more than a true to type Leo. This is where parents need to take control of the situation and exercise some discipline because if this tendency is allowed to go unchecked the child can become absolutely obnoxious.

Leo likes to be number one and usually wants the best of everything. However, if this child receives too much too easily it will not be valued nor appreciated. Therefore, parents, should educate their little one from a very early age about the dangers of easy come, easy go.

Leo is known as the Royal Star Sign because its ruler the Sun is the King of the Solar System, so during the whole lifetime from childhood through adulthood to old age this person will be like a ray of sunshine, bringing joy, light and some degree of splendour, pomp and ceremony wherever he or she goes.

This child is impressed by success, strength, prestige and self confidence in others, so never let your fears and weaknesses become obvious.

VIRGO CHILD (August 24 to September 23)

Virgo being one of the earth signs is very practical, realistic and down to earth. So you can be sure that this child will not live in a world of fantasy and day dreams. He or she will always appreciate good common sense and needs to have a logical explanation for all the how's when's where's and why's of life's activieis and experiences.

Mecury (the planet of the intelect) rules Virgo. So this child has a keen, sharp, analytical mind and he or she will always reason things out in a rational, intelligent kind of way, Therefore, a Virgoan is usually of diligent student and develops into a reliable, responsible citizen. This star sign is certainly the hallmark of a perfectionist who likes everything to be done carefully, properly and accurately. Method, order and system also belong to Virgo, so a messy household will subconsiously distrub this child. Attention to detail and a natural ability to work with small items are typical of this star sign. Because of this he or she notices all the little things there is also an inborn critical faculty, don't be surprised if your child often picks faults in various ways and in other people.

Virgo is inclined to build a protective shell, so unless parents, by example, encourage to feelings and emotions , the love nature will gradually become more and more reserved, conservative, very cool and even a little inhibited.

Having a practical, useful, attainable purpose in life is of paramount importance to a Virgoan, so parents should encourage the child to do some little chores around the house. You can be sure they will be done with a fair degree of perfection.

Because the nature is quiet reserved, modest and timid this child will not seek the limelight.

LIBRA CHILD (September 24 to October 23)

Venus (the mythological goddess of love and beauty) is the ruler of Libra . Here is one reason why a son or daughter of this star sign has a friently, affectionate, appealing nature which is popular with most people. Libra is the hallmark of peace, harmony, tranquality and equilibrium, so for the child to be happy it is absolutely essential that the home environment reflects these qualities. There is nothing which will upset a Libran more than arguments, aggression, tension, conflicts and a nasty atmosphere, especially when this involves the family, loved ones and close personal relationship.

Artistry of all kinds has an affinity with Libra, so your child may have a talent for such things as music, painting, dancing, makup, dress making or other creative activities. Harmonious sounds and colours appeal to this star sign so make sure that the toy cupboard contains items such as paints, coloured play things, a toy sewing machine or piano and other bits and pieces which will cater for any artistic talents. Make the child's room as attractive as possible because anything ugly or discordant will have a disturbing effect on his or her sense.

Libra is the sign of partnership, so most people born during this period need someone with whom they can share all of life's ingredients. Therefore, allow your child to have a special playmate because he or she will not feel happy being alone for too long.

If parents begin at an early age it will not be difficult to teach their child to be polite and well mannered, a courteous, gentle approach to others comes naturally to a Libran, who will often go out of his her way to please people. A difficult lesson will come later in life with the discovery that it is impossible to please everyone all the time.

SCORPIO CHILD (October 24 to November 22)

Because Scorpio is one of the water signs this child is intensely emotional with very deep feelings. However, like many facets of the Scorpio nature these feelings and emotions are oten well concealed; there is a strong desire to keep things secret rather than disclose too much to others. Don't be surprised if your child hides some of his or her little treasure in place which you don't know about. This youngster will thoroughly enjoy investigating and ferreting things out, because anything secret, mysterious or hidden holds a special fascination. Therefore, parents should double check for danger sports around the house were the child could be at risk.

Mars (the mythological god of war) and Pluto (lord of the under world and the symbol of the two extremes- the greatest depths and the supreme heights) are the rulers of Scorpio, so there is certainly nothing wishy-washy about your child. He or she will sometimes be a perfect saint and at other a little devil. There are no half measures for this star sign. So in relationships he or she can either love or hate with equal intensity.

When it comes to overcoming an obstacle or an opponent, Scorpio can be ruthless and invincible and since this star sign endows your child with geat will power, fortitude and determination, he or she will never surrender nor give up until the goal or battle is won. In adult life this inner strength will be a great asset for achieving success. One of the negative aspects of Scorpio is a tendency to be cruel and destructive, so if you see your child tormenting another child, a pet or smashing toys, try to take positive action to quash these nasty characteristics.

The star sign gives an intuitive, perceptive and even psychic awareness fo your child will always sense the reality behind the facade.

SAGITTARIUS CHILD (November 23 to December 21)

Sagittarius is one of the active, out going, extrovert fire signs and since it is also ruled by Jupiter (the planet of expansion, success, joy and good fortune) your child will be a bundle of energy, enthusiasm, optimism, fun and has every chance of living a full, satisfying, busy life.

This is not a moody, depressing star sign, so it takes a lot to get a Sagittarian down and even when this does happen he or she will soon bounce back again, Even in times of trouble, Jupiter's lucky influence means that something beneficial will come along to save the day and the person will somehow manage to land on his or her feet.

Sagittarius is the hallmark of freedom and independence, so your child will not feel happy when living, playing or working in confined areas or cramped, restrictive conditions. A Sagittarian needs a taste of the wide open spaces where there is plenty of room to move, so parents should take this child out into the country for such things as bush walking, riding, camping, picnicking and having some free and easy fun.

In some ways this person no matter at what age, wants to be a free spirit so he or she will not take kindly to parental control and discipline which usually comes in the form of "you must not do" however you should tactfully educate your child to accept the limitations and responsibilities whch life, society and the law demands, otherwise he or she may resent a situation in adulthood where ties and restrictions apply. If this acceptance is not achieved it could jeopardise a marriage or cause problems in the sphere of work.

This star sign will make your child generous, warm hearted, exuberant, friendly, always optimistic, straight forward- even to the point of being abrupt or a Jack Blunt, but with a good sense of humour.

CAPRICORN CHILD (December 22 to January 21)

Being one of the earth signs, Capricorn is very cautious, realistic, practical, conservative and likes to get down to basics. Since Saturn (the ruler of Capricorn) is the symbol of maturity, responsibility, austerity and wisdom gained through experienced, your child is a serious minded person who is likely to have an old head on young shoulders. He or she is reserved and some what modest and retiring rather than effervescent and demonstrative. There is not a great deal of interest in things which are superficial or frivolous because Capricorn is equipped to deal with fundamental or mature matters. You will even notice that your child seems to have an affinity for older people.

This star sign is the hallmark of duty and responsibility so in a large family it is often the Capricorn son or daughter who is landed with the job of taking care of the other children. This can be just one of many reasons why he or she frequently misses out on much of normal childhood fun and therefore grows up at an early age.

Fire, air and water can all move quickly, whereas earth is static. How ever, it also typifies stability and security, two things which a Capricornian will strive to achieve "Slow but sure" is the star sign's motto and since there is a real capacity for persistence, endurance and perserevance once this child decides that he or she wants to do or have something, there will be no giving up until the objective is achieved, no matter how long it takes.

Capricorn does not often act spontaneously but prefers to plan well ahead so that everything can be done carefully and properly. Those who are so diligent and conscientious only feel a sense of satisfaction when something is well done.

Here is a person who cannot tolerate waste or extravagance.

AQUARIUS CHILD (January 22 to February 21)

Aquarius is one of the most unusual, unpredictable, independent and enigmatic signs of the Zodiac and since Uranus, its ruling planet, is the symbol of all that is original, unique, unorthodox, sudden, surprising, erratic and rebellious, your child will not always fit into the standard mould of what is considered to be conventional, traditional, ordinary, normal and predictable, Uranus is outside the orbit of conventional Saturn and in some ways Aquariums are out sides because they are like free spirits who are untameable and uncatchable. Many are non conformists (or even rebels) who like to do their own thing, without being beholden to anyone. Consequently, the more conservative members of society find it very difficult and sometimes imposible to really undestand what makes an Aquarian tick. The paradox is that they are happy to conform when they are not forced to do so.

Parents will have to be extremely diplomatic in the way in which they administer discipline and guidance.

This child of Aquarius has a high degree of intelligence (often ahead of its time) with a wide range of interests. In some things he or she will have fixed ideas; the more you try to chance those opinions the more inflexible the mind will become.

This star sign gives a broad minded outlook which encompasses a wide range of interests such as humanitarian interest, social issuesers, space, astrology or electronics.

Aquarians are friendly and sociable and they are often more at ease when mixing with large numbers of people such as clubs, groups and friends rather than being restricted to the company of one person for long periods. Sometimes the Aquarian will decide to go it solo. In other words, you never quite know what an Aquarian will do.

PISCES CHILD (February 22 to March 20)

Whether developed and active or latent but dormant, the intuitive and psychic faculties are stronger in Pisces than in any other star sign. Therefore, parents of this child should be aware that he or she will often have hunches, know things without a word being spoken, experience telepathy and E.S.P. in various ways, and at times seem to be in an other world. Because of these and other strange, unfathomable qualities, it is almost impossible to completely known and understand a true Piscean person, young or old. Once of the reasons for this is that Neptune which reigns over this star sign is as deep, mysterious and unplumbed as the sea.

This child is extremely sensitive, so if upset or the feelings are hurt he or she will withdraw into a private, secret inner world where no one can enter. Because there is this strange ability to link up with another dimension of consiciousness, some Piscean children find it difficult to differentiate between fact and fantasy.

Pisces is guided by instinct, intuition and feelings rather than by logic, rules and cold, hard facts, So don't expect your child (even in adulthood) to have a logical, practical or rational reason for many of the things he or she does.

Quite frequently this star sign lives in a world of vivid imagination. Pisces is super sensitive and highly impressionable, making your child very responsive and receptive to external influences. Therefore parents should realise that it is of paramount importance that this sensitive child should only mix with people whose ideas, interests, motives and way of life are of an exemplary nature. Your child will unconsciously imitate the people he or she likes, so if the company is of a high calibre, some of it will be copied. However, the same rule will apply to bad company.

26

Q. A. ON PRE-SCHOOL SAFETY

Q. Which dangers should I be aware of now my child is getting older ?

Ans. You need to be aware that your child is becoming more independent and capable, but still has a limited sense of danger. He may even think he is immortal and invincible, like a cartoon character. Make sure windows and doors are safe, keep poisonous substances locked away and start teaching him basic road-safety awareness.

Q. How can I teach my child about safety ?

Ans. When you're doing things with him in the kitchen or the garden, give him a running commentary. For example, if you are in the kitchen making a cake you can tell him in a positive way about the importance of being careful with kitchen utensils and hot ovens, and show him that you are putting these precautions into practice. Conversely, if he sees you put a knife into your mouth to lick it, don't be surprised if he copies you.

Q. How can I keep my child safe and still let him be independent?

Ans. As you can't protect your child all the time but you can reduce risks and avoid exposing him to unnecessary hazards. Let him become more independent in controlled circumstances. For instance, a child can learn to handle small tools such as a screwdriver or hammer under close supervision. Teach him good safety habits and try to explain why the safety rules are important, so that he can apply the guidelines in other situations.

Q. What should I tell my child about talking to strangers?

Ans. Avoid scare tactics - your child must learn safety without fear. Explain to him that not all strangers are bad, but that he should not talk to strangers or accept anything from a stranger. If someone is simply returning something that belongs to the child, he should get no closer than an arm's length away. Tell your child that he must never go anywhere with a stranger. This is especially important if your child always does as you say. On the whole, it is perfectly safe for him to talk to grown-ups he knows well.

Q. How can I protect my child against sexual abuse?

Ans. As well as never going anywhere with a stranger, tell your child not to keep a secret, especially if someone asks him to. If someone says or does something in a way he doesn't like, he should tell the person to stop and then tell you. No stranger should touch his body, especially not his private parts (if he asks, these are the parts covered by a swimsuit) - with obvious exceptions, like visiting the doctor.

Q. My son plays rough games with his friends. How can I keep him safe?

Ans. Little boys enjoy very physical forms of play but don't always have much common sense. Make sure they don't play with dangerous objects, such as pieces of metal or sharp sticks and supervise their play, for your child's sake and that of his friends. If it gets too rough, break it up at intervals for a snack or a drink before the situation gets totally out of hand.

Q. Should I take anything with me when I'm out with my child?

Ans. Yes, but how much depends on how long you will be out. You may even need food and drink (snacks or a meal, or both) and something to entertain him with. Tie a toy, using a short ribbon no longer than 20 cm (8 in), onto his buggy or his car seat, so that he can't lose it-or throw it at you when you are driving. A potty (or change of nappy) is also a good idea. Take his changing bag, filled with basic essentials. If he suffers from motion sickness, you'll need a plastic bag, some paper towels and a change of clothes.

Q. Where can I change my baby's nappy when we are out on a trip?

Ans. Most departmental stores, supermarkets and motorway service stations provide nappy-changing facilities. Unfortunately these are usually in the ladies' changing room, although some places have a family room, which is more convenient for fathers. Otherwise, use the luggage shelf of the car or the car seats if out in the car. If you are desperate, find a quiet spot in a park.

Q. How can I feed my baby when we are out and about?

Ans. You can stop and feed your baby almost anywhere as long as it is hygienic. Depending on the weather, you can breast-fed, bottle-feed or give solid food on a park bench. All you need is his food, a spoon, a bib and paper towels to mop up spills. Take a couple of plastic bags with you for used items. Most restaurants will happily heat up baby food for you and many have highchairs. Alternatively, you can restrain your baby by securing a harness to an ordinary chair - add a booster seat, and you have a highchair.

Q. How can I keep my baby contented on long journeys?

Ans. Make sure your baby is fed and changed before you start the journey. With luck he will fall asleep in the car, and soothing music may help. Failing that, provide a toy or two in case he doesn't sleep. Most babies are happy with a string of beads stretched out across the baby seat, a small soft toy or a board book. If the toy is attached to the car seat, you won't have to keep picking it up.

27

DIABETES IN CHILDREN

If a child is diagnosed for diabetes, it is an occasion for utmost worry-first for the parents and then for the child who is subjected to many a restriction to which he is not formerly accustomed. Diabetes is of two types :

Diabetes Ispidus

When there is profuse and frequent flow of urine. This condition is not serious as there is no sugar in urine or blood, and is manageable quite easily. The child passes large quantities of urine after short intervals and gets weaker and tired.

Diabetes Mellitus

Of the two types, it is the most disturbing aspect of diabetes when, in addition the aforesaid symptoms, there is presence of sugar in urine and blood. First there is presence of sugar in blood but later on when blood sugar is not controlled, the sugar content passes in to urine also.

Heredity Factor

Heredity factor is said to be a potent factor in causing diabetes in the offspring. It is not true that if a mother is diabetic, her child would also be a born diabetic. The only factor worth recognition is that child of a diabetic mother is more exposed to onset of diabetes but it is not, at all, necessary that a diabetic mother's child will also be born as a diabetic. Due to use of certain drugs during pregnancy, the mother may develop diabetic symptoms but if detected and treated in time, she can be freed from diabetes and its effects. But those mothers, who are confirmed diabetics before conception and remain so even during the course of pregnancy, are most likely to pass on this symptom to their off spring. The reason being that the foetus is nourished by the food which pregnant woman consumes.

It is simply a metabolic disorder. The fact of the matter remains that children of diabetic parent may or may not be born as diabetics, but 'Risk Factor' still looms largely on them. On the other hand non-diabetic parents may have diabetic children. The least the diabetic parents can do is to guide their children about factors that are held to be causatives of this malady as 'Forewarned child becomes a forearmed child'. This applied especially to either or both the diabetic parents who are indolent, inactive, lead a sedentary life, avoid any physical activity, eat frequently and in huge quantities, consume carbohydrates in plenty, do not use fibre, eat less of leafy and green vegetables. In short they do not perform any physical activity which could enable them to burn / expend the calories generated through indiscreet food consumption.

Problems in Treating the Diabetic Child

- ☞ If too many dietary restrictions are imposed, the child's growth pattern will be adversely affected and, thus, recoil on his mental and physical development.

- If carbohydrates, proteins, and fats are totally withdrawn or even if partially tapered, his all-round progress will be disturbed and he may lack in physical activity, studies, games and other extracurricular activities.
- It is an uphill task to adjust dosage of insulin and quantity of food intake.
- Insulin injection is a painful experience for the child and the child resists and avoids such injections and is, generally, not able to keep pace with diet and insulin injections.
- Dosage of insulin is required to be adjusted and moderated as per rise of fall in the sugar level which rquired to be simultaneously adjusted with diet.
- If diet is not taken immdiately after the insulin injection, sugar level is bound to fall rather suddenly.
- If insulin injection is not taken at the designatd time and in recommended dosage, blood sugar level will rise.
- Sudden rise or fall in blood sugar level will interfere with the child's normal activity, studies, games and other allied extra curricular activities. In short, his entire routine will get disturbed.
- Close and constant monitoring is required in relation to insulin diet and activity which a child finds difficult to adhere to.

It is the duty of parents to keep in mind on the above mentioned problems. It is to be known that diabetes is fully manageable, treatable and controllable but cannot be cured once forever; 'once a diabetic, always a diabetic should be borne in mind. It is like blood pressure which also can be controlled but never cured. The parents should always cheer up the child and never scare him nor potray a depressing picture. Try to enliven and keep up his spirits, thereby boosting his self-confidence and morale. Do not scar the child nor impose any unncessary restrictions on diet and activity nor interference with his studies.

TREATMENT

A patient has no option but to depend upon insulin - as far as a child or an adult is concerned, though elderly persons can be managed by oral antiglycaemic drums which are easier to manage. As far as proper treatment is concerned, patient should be kept under supervision of a doctor who is the only right person to advise on adjustement of insulin dosage and diet. Keeping all such considerations in view, I am avoiding to suggest any mode of treatment and diet which aspects ought to be conductd by a doctor, though follow up action is to be performed by the parents and the child.

If diabetes is not controlled in time and allowed to prolong, following complications may arise :

1. Late healing of wounds and apparance of ulcers.
2. Digstive disorders.
3. Hardening of blood vessls (Arteriosclerosis).
4. Damage to Peripheral Nerves (Peripheral diabetic neuropathy).
5. Damag to kidneys and hardening of soft tissues (Diabetic Nephropathy).
6. Damage to eye-sight (Particularly damage to retina called Retinopathy).
7. Skin problems like boils, pimples, rough skin, rashes, pruritis, urticaria etc.

8. Loose teeth and spongy gums.
9. Impotency, sterility, phimosis ro paraphimosis.

Reactions of Insulin

Primary Symptoms (Hypoglycaemia)

1. Sudden fall in sugar level.
2. Unconsciousness or / and listlessness.
3. Rapid pulsation of heart.
4. Excessive hunger.
5. Trembling, convulsions.
6. Sinking of body energy to its lowest.
7. Staggering gate and darkness beefore eyes.
8. Short-term memory failure, mental instability, disorientation, forgetfullness.

Secondary Symptoms

1. Unbearable itching (Pruritis), hives / urticaria.
2. Nausea, vomiting and loose motions.
3. Bloating of abdomen.
4. Black/dark rings or spots around eyes or/and on skin.
5. Shedding of fat and general run-down condition.
6. In some cases patients put on extra weight even.

Hypoglycemia can be easily managed by ingesting sugar-rich beverages or dissolving sugar or sugar cubes in water which will remove the above-mentiond complications. The diabetics are advised to keep some amount of sugar with them, preferably dissolved in water, as a handy tool to meet emergent situations. Even sweet bisucits, toffees, sweets, chocolates should be kept in readiness to meet such sudden situations.

28
TREATMENT THROUGH AYURVEDA

Ayurveda is a well estabished science which is non harming to children.

Fever

Ayurveda is an ancient Indian Science providing treatment by herbs and refined chemicals.

Praval Bhasma - 50-60 mg (for children aged 1-2 years with milk will quell general fever but, when fever is due to cough, cold and dyspepsia, give 15 mg with milk. Fever due to head can be brought down by Paracetamol (¼-½ Tsp - Paed dose - or 50 - 100 mg of aspirin) soluble. If 15-25 mg of Abhrak Bhasma is given ½-1 hour before anticipated time of fever, it won't let fever surface occur - it will also relieve symptoms of cough. Septrin tablets of Baidyanath are also good.

Cough

If cough is dry and sputum is difficult to expel, mix 125 mg each of parched and pulverised powder of Alum and Borax and mix with honey which the child should like (give this 3-

4 times daily). It will moisten and loose the phlegm and help it to expectorate, normalise respiration and relieve cough. It is also useful in tonsillitis.

If phlegm is white, give parched borax powder and Abhrak Bhasma 15-20 mg (mixed with honey)3-4 times daily. Anand Bhairava Rasa (15-20 mg) may also be given for the same purpose (2-3 times daily).

Pain in Ribs

Prepare a liniment / rubbing oil by mixing heeng (Asafoetida) and garlic. Massage this oil over the affected rib-area 2-3 times daily. In addition give also Abhrak Bhasma (5-10 mg) with milk or honey. It will not only remove pain but also remove swelling.

Abdominal / Stomach Pain

This is also known as colic. Mix asafoetida, fried harar and table salt with milk or honey or apply Amritdhara locally over navel and adjoining area. It can also be given in 2 drop doses with a lump of sugar or mixed with milk. As a supportive measure, the child should be laid on his stomach sid and gently patted-it will also expel trapped wind and provide relief to the child.

Pain in the Ear

Fry 4-5 cloves of garlic and 25-30 gms of asafoetida in mustard oil. Boil and let it cool down. Drop 2 -3 drops in the painful ear. Alternatively 3-4 drops of doctor's brandy (slighthly heated in winter) should be inserted into the painful ear. Even 2-3 drops of turpentine oil used as ear-drops or extracted juice of onion and some alum (red colour) should be mixed together to yield the relieving effect. But do not probe anything into the ear, as it (It is better to consult an ENT Specialist) may cause infection and aggravate pain.

Stomatitis

This condition arises due to reddening of mucus surface in the mouth when the child refuses to be fed and cries when any attempt is made to feed him. There may also be white patches on sub mucus portion. Mix parched alum, Papparia Kattha, and powder of cardamom with honey and apply over the infected site or else parchd suhaga, alum powder or kattha and kabab cheeni should be mixed with honey or ghee (pure) and applied locally, as indicated above.

Pain in Eyes and Redness

I am of the opinion that most of the children are quite sensitive to ayurvedic medicines if used as eye drops. Pure rose water is, by far, the best effective and harmless device 1-2 drop into each eye, 3-4 times daily and also wash the eyes with weak lotion of boric acid. Some people suggest use of alum with rose / plain water but I will advise you to get in touch with a vaidya for proper and harmless treatment.

Diarrhoea

Tyr Nar. Kachoor - 15-20 gms and mix it with mother's / cow's milk and taken thrice daily - will stop green loose motions or levy 125 mg Kamaraja Rasa with milk or substitute this Rasa with Pravala Bhasma (125 mg) with milk and honey (equal quantity of both) and give either of the comibnations 6 hourly.

If the above mentioned combinations fail to yield any relief give 15-25 mg of Anand Bhariava or Sanjeevani by mixing with honey and mother's or cow's milk. It will stop loose motion quite quickly. Consult your vaidya about Rasa Peepari for this disorder. In any case, try to maintain sodium-water-balance in the body and give only boiled water (when it has cooled) or juice of pomegranate (1-2 tsp thrice).

Constipation

It is considered as the chief causative of host of other diseases. Constipation has direct effect on metabolism. Unsuitable, stale, putrid diet is held to responsible for this problem. Mix powders of Alua Usari Revand 6 gms each, fried heeng 2 gm and prepare a thick paste so that pills of 10-15 mg could be processed. Give one such pill to the infant with mother's milk - it will expel trapped milk and ease constipation or give powder or parched Suhaga 1 gm, Usari Revand 500 mg and serve with milk to regulate bowels or give 10-15 mg of Anand Bhaairava Rasa with water or milk.

Worms

Extracted juice of fresh onion (1 gm) + 10-15 mg of heeng should be given with water in the morning and evening - it will expel worms. Apply locally paste of roots of Indrayan and Bakayan over the stomach, to derive desired benefit, or prepare a paste of roots of Vaya Vidang and Kabela, adding some amount of fried heeng. Before giving this compound, give jaggery (Gur) first. It will also expel worms. Some people suggest taking of two half-cut pieces of ripe tomato, sprinkling powder of black pepper for being taken in the morning on empty stomach.

To Restore Free Flow of Urine

This is a dangerous condition and must not be handled by a layman but by a vaidya only. The medicines suggested should serve as a guideline only and not used without proper guidance and monitoring of a vaidya. When no urine is passed, it is still a graver situation and calls for immediate hospitalisation. Parents who are syphilitic or had been so but had not been declared 'negative' should be extra careful. Generally, retention of urine is attributed to some obstructive pathology like stone in the urinary tract, some urinary infection. Without going into clinical details, use of catheter is the only possible alternative or consult some surgeon but do not leave anything to chance. If urinary flow is not free and urine is expelled in drops, with much pain and tenesmus or blood/pus is also passed, it points to some sort of obstruction in the urinary passage. Scanty urine in summer or during diarrhoea or when water intake is not sufficient to meet every body's normal demands, such situation may surface.

Bal Roga Janam Ghutti

Take an equal quantity Zahar Mohra salai, Hajrul Yahood, Dariyai Narial, yellow Harar, Bansholochan, Peepal, Ilayachi, Jaiphal, Kesar, Gulab ke phool and finely pound all the ingredients. Process pills to the weight of 10-15 mg. Dissolve a pill in mother's milk and given evening and morning. It is said to be beneficial in fever, (intense) thirst, loos motions, vomiting of milk and other diseases which are specially attributed to infancy stage. This formulation is said to be quite useful.

Formulations to Cure Marasmus

Majeeth 60 gms, Challera Sugandh wala and Nagarmotha (each 22-25 gm), Haldi 25 gms, Laung, Saunth Tej, jaiphal, Daru Haldi, Sliced pieces of ginger, Peepal - 6 gms each, Kachoor 50 gms, Sandalwood powder, Lal chandan 12 gms each, Kapur (Camphor) 3 gms - boil all the mentioned ingredients in water (in 1.25 litres), When the water content is reduced to 1 kg, mix ½ litre Til oil to it and boil until entire quantity of water evaporates and only oil is left behind. After this, mix in Lal Ratanjyot in the oil and remove from fire. After removing from fire put in 4-6 tablets of Camphor and when the liquid cools down, bottle the contents and tighten securely with a cork or stopper. Finally prepared oil is said to remove fever, pains and aches in the body, shrivelling of skin, weakness and will make muscles and bones healthy, tough and full of strength.

Mulethi 6 gms, Ilayachi, Dalchini, Tulsi leaves (2 gms each), Banshlochan 3 gms, Kesar 250 gms, sugar candy equivalent to half the weight of above-mentioned ingredients-all the ingredients may be levied and reduced to paste form in juice of Tulsi leaves and prepare pills of 125 mg each. A pill may be dissolved with mother's milk and given to the infant 3-4 times daily to get rid of infantile marasmus.

Root of Patharchata 500 mg may be rubbed in mother's milk and 300 mg black pepper powder added to it. It should be served to a child for 3 days (one dose daily) and is said to cure marasmus.

Note: Quantities mentioned above and down below or in other cases are simply indications only and may be adjusted in consultation with a vaidya, as also frequency of dosage.

Bal Sanjeevan Ark

Saunf, Ajwain, Vaiviranta (2 gms each), Peepal, Parched borax, Nausadar, Marorh Phali, Munakka-12 gms each, Makoy 125 mg, Indra Jau 250 mg, Sanai Mulethi, Harar, kachoor, Laung, Mangore, Amaltas-60 gms each. Boil all the said ingredients, (after reducing all of them into a powder form) in 10 kgs water. When the contents are reduced to 1¼ kgs, put in Kesar 400 mg and sugar candy 400 gms all boil again. Remove from fire and let it cool, after which the contents should be bottled and corked. The resultant product, so procured, is said to make weak and marasmic children stronger, removes fever, cough, stomach and digestion related disorders, including green or yellow loose stools.

Kasturi Vati

Jaiphal, Sheetal Cheeni, Tej, Laung, llayaichi, Banshlochan, Peepal - 6 gms each. Reduce all the ingredients to powder form and then add 3 gms and Kasturi (Musk) 1 gm and prepare a suitable thick paste to process pills of 125 mg each. Give a pill with mother's milk 2-3 times daily to cure fever, cough, cold, curdling and vomiting of milk, greenish loose stools, flu etc. It should preferably be used in winter and cold but rarely in summer and hot conditions.

Ras Peepari

Process kajali from purified mercury and purified sulphur (6 gms) each after which add 3 gms each of powdered Heeng (fried). Peepal, Saunth, Tej, Jaiphal, Kesar (fried), Suhaga, rock(red) Salt, fried laung, Ateesa, Ajwain, Vaivaringa, Kakkarsinghi and mix with Kakali and process pills of 125 mg each. It is said to be useful when the child is suffering from cold, fever, cough, nasal discharge, flu, milk vomiting, green and loose motions, and other stomach and digestion related disorders. One pill should be dissolved in mothers or cow's milk and given 2-3 times daily. This preparation is said to serve both as a preventive and curative device. It will also benefit during fever (due to cold conditions and coryza and catarrh).

29

BIOCHEMICAL COMBINATIONS FOR CHILDREN

There are 28 combination componds of biochemic remedies which are detailed hereunder with main symptoms for which each one should be used. These combinations are numerically numbered.

Before purchasing any biochemic combinations, make sure that only products of standard homeo companies are purchased (eg. WSI, SBL, Ralson, Bakson, Bioforce etc.)

Biochemic Compounds

Number-1	Anaemia
Number-2	Asthma
Number-3	Colic
Number-4	Constipation
Number-5	Coryza
Number-6	Cough, cold and Catarrh
Number-7	Diabetes
Number-8	Diarrhoea

Number-9	Dysentery
Number-10	Enlarged Tonsils
Number-11	Fever
Number-12	Headache
Number-13	Leucorrhoea
Number-14	Measles
Number-15	Menstruation Troubles
Number-16	Nervous Exhaustion
Number-17	Piles
Number-18	Pyorrhoea
Number-19	Rheumatism
Number-20	Skin Diseases
Number-21	Teething troubles of Children
Number-22	Scrofula
Number-23	Toothache
Number-24	Tonic for Nerves and Brain
Number-25	Acidity, Flatulence and Indigestion
Number-26	Easy Dilivery/Parturition
Number-27	Lack of Vitality
Number-28	General Tonic

Dosage for children and adults have been mentioned on each combination but in emergent situations like cholera, diarrhoea, colic, flatulence, fever etc dosage may be repeated with greater frequency but quantity of dose will, however, remain the same. In case of any confusion or difficulty a Homeopthic physician should be consulted.

Mostly used Biochemic Combination No. 21 (Teething Troubles)

These tablets help to build up general health of the baby and also keep him free from most of the health problems which normally occur during dentition period. It is a combination of Ferrum Phos and Calcarea Phos which in combined form, proves more effective and efficacious due to addition of Ferrum Phos. Mothers generally prefer to use Calcarea Phos but, in my view, this combination should be preferred in comparison to single use of Calcarea Phos. If these tablets are used regularly (from the anticipated time of cutting teeth) until your child can be relieved from the agony of dentition problems.

30
HOMOEOPATHIC TREATMENT ON THE BASIS OF WEEPING

- ☞ Weeps when he wants to walk in fever : Bryonia.
- ☞ Weeps all the night but sleeps durnig the day time. Jalapa.
- ☞ Grasps and catches hold of the rib due to fear of falling down and does not sleep: Borax
- ☞ Weeps profusely at the time of birth. Medorrh.
- ☞ Weeps as if frightened as from seeing some horible object: Stramonium.
- ☞ Weeps due to colic or abdominal pain: Cuprum Me, Mag Phos.
- ☞ Weeps and afraid to breath: Belladonna.
- ☞ Weeps due to gripes for an hour after taking milkfeed: Nux Vomica.
- ☞ Is obstinate and demands odd things but quietens only when demanded and desired thing is given to him: Chamomilla.
- ☞ Weeps from 4 am to 9 pm bores his feet into pubes, tenesmus while passing stool but excreta is extremely hard and passed in minimal quantity: Colo cynth.

- Weeps continuosly day and night: Psorinum.
- Sleep well upto sunrise but continuses to weep till noon time: Calcarea Carb.
- Weeps due to locking up of wind in the stomach (in relation to cyanosis of whole body): Calc.Carb.
- Bores his head into the pillow and polaces his hand behind his head: Bryonia.
- Suddenly weeps and suddenly stops Belladonna.
- Weeps while being forcibly fed by mother: Calc Phos.
- Weeps due to some apparent and visible cause: Causticum.
- Weeps due to worms distended abdomen alongwith pain in the stomach: Staphysagria.
- Weeps due to ill- effects of anger: Aconite.
- Weeps due to retarded growth of limbs: Lyco, Magn. Mur
- Weeps due to fear of going down: Borax.
- Weeps due to fear of movement. Wishes to be carried in are: Rhus Tox, Cina
- Child cries in pauses (not continuously) : Apis.
- Child cries in a heart-rending voice: Cuprum Met.
- Child cries during thc time of sleep: Cina.
- Child cries during/at the time of teething: Aethusa, Natum Mur, Mag, Phos.
- Child cries and continues to cry even when looked up casually and gets up agitated after sleep: Antim.Tart.
- Child passed blood from Nose: Tebinthina.
- Does not wish to feed with milk. Cod liver Oil.

- ☞ Child sees odd thing and weeps: Aethusa.
- ☞ Child weeps unless holded: Chamom.

Note: Initially, if you find any symptom, give single medicine in 30 potency, one or two drops, thrice a day in one spoon of water. If there is no relief, consult a qualified, experienced homoeopathic physician.

31

COMPLEMENTARY THERAPIES USED FOR CHILDREN

There are many therapies used for children. The most common of these include:

Ostpopathy

A system of manipulation. The method most frequently used to treat children is cranial osteopathy.

Homeopathy

Treatment is based on the theory a substance, that in large doses causes specific symptoms will in tiny doses relieve the same symptoms.

Herbal Medicine

The use of the active medicinal constituents of plants' Chinese herbal medicine can be effective for childhood eczema.

Aromatherapy

Using herbal oils (called essential oils) mixed into a massage oil inhaled as vapour using a special burner.

Accupressure

Pressure on certain points by thumb or index fingure.

How can Aromatherapy help children ?

Although there is little objective evidence, aromatherapy can sometimes be effective for:

- ☞ minor cuts and grazes (tea plant oil)
- ☞ catarrh (lemonand ucalyptus oil)
- ☞ chicken-pox (lavender and tea plant oil)
- ☞ headlice (a blend of tea plant, rose, eucalyptus, lemon, lavender and geranium oils)
- ☞ nappy rash (tea plant oil used as an antiseptic, rinse when washing cloth nappies)
- ☞ sleep problems (usually lavender oil).

Essential oils are diluted in a base oils and either applied to the affected area, used in massage or inhaled as vapour. When using aromatherapy make sure that the oil is suitable for a child and that she does not taste or swallow it oils are all very strong and some of them are toxic.

32

GENERAL CAUTION ON ADMINISTRATION OF MEDICINES

- Complete entire course of preventive vaccinations and do not skip over or delay.
- Never give any medicine on empty stomach or soon after feeding nor disturb a child when he is asleep, continues to sleep.
- Never exceed the stated and recommended dose nor give are adult dose to a child. Give only paedriatic preparation.
- Stop use of medicine when the child has fully recovred but some medicines are to be given for a specific period, hence do not cut short the treatment mid-way.
- Give medicines either dissolved in water or with some palatable vehicle but avoid giving tablets straightway on tongue as they might gag him or cause respiration problems.
- Capsuled medicines generally adhere and stick to soft palate or throat and, thus, may choke him, hence use liquid / tablet form instead.

- ☞ Do not mix any medicine with child's feed. In some cases some medicines may be mixed with mother's milk (if the child is breast-fed) and then given but follow your doctor's advice.
- ☞ Do not insert any eye drop or ear drop without consulting a physician nor use any corticosteroid preparations as your ear drop or as an ointment.
- ☞ Be careful to apply only baby cream, baby soap, baby oil and never use any other soap, shampoo, cream or oil which the elders use.
- ☞ In nausea and vomiting, avoid giving any feed as the child may vomit the same.
- ☞ Do not use too hot or too cold a vehicle (like water) while giving any medicine.

The list does not end here and there are many other cautions which elders know by their experience.

33

LIFE AS A WORKING PARENT

There are lots of advantages for working mothers–like feeling independent, extra stimulation derived from work, even the fact that you and your child may appreciate each other all the more for spending less time together.

But there's a price : your free time. For most working time flies past goes–not on you–but on your child and instead of coming home from work and collapsing into a chair with a drink, your baby will be wanting your individend attention. It's not good pretending this will be a breeze. It won't. But forewarned is forearmed and your aim now is to make life as easy as possible, especially during the first three months of adjusting to your dual role. To do this, you need :

☞ A husband who is prepared to share the child and the housework. The key word here is share. You want a partner in this project not someone who changes the odd nappy now and then. The best approach is to discuss this during your pregnancy and extract and agreement to share child care and domestic chores (which he should preferably sign in blood or have tattooed indelibly across his wrist).

It's a sad fact of life that condition on the home front haven't kept up with advances in the work-place and many women still end up doing the major share at home. This is a real health hazard.

To Lighten the Domestic Load

- A good rule to live by for the first few months is Do Nothing Unless It's Absolutely Necessary. Ration your resources to cope with work and the baby. Most working mothers will tell you they quickly learn to turn a blind eye to dust and less-than-perfect housekeeping. Plan one supermarket expedition once a fortnight or once a month rather than weekly. It saves a lot of time and energy. Use shops that deliver telephone orders.
- Get help with leaning or ironing - if you can afford it. This might seem like an outrageous luxury, but is a good investment in your well being. it might be worth going without something else so as to afford it in those first few hectic weeks of juggling job and baby. It's a great relief to wake (or be woken up.) on Saturday morning, knowing someone else has taken care of the major chores.
- Rest as much as you can. Even if the baby is sleeping through the night, you may still have to contend with broken sleep due to wet nappies and teething pangs. Make a deal with your partner that you each get to sleep in on one weekend morning while the other looks after the baby. Use times why the baby sleeps on weekends to rest yourself-lying down with a good books makes more sense than doing all the house cleaning.
- A good diet and exercises. Convenience food might be very tempting at this stage, but if you adopt, any bad

eating habits you'll short-change yourself on the nutrients you need to stay on top. The fitter you are the more stamina you'll have to cope, so exercise when you can - lunch time walks on work-days, perhaps, or long walks with the stroller on weekends.

☞ Limit your work responsibilities. Of course you'll want to do your job well, but during these early months isn't the time to take on extra commitments that aren't strictly necessary.

☞ A last word about guilt. Be prepared to feel guilty-almost furtive, even -- the first time you leave your baby in child care. You'll find the guilt fades once you see how happy your baby can be in the company of other people.

As well as helping you get on with the job without worrying, good child care offers children real benefits like fresh experiences, companionships and help in relating to other people.

34

HOW TO TAKE THE BEST PHOTOGRAPHS OF YOUR BABY

A wonderful photograph can happen at any time but you have to be alert and patient. It's most important to remember your baby will give you little or no assistance.

If he isn't in a good mood don't force the issue or the camera will be associated with a bad experience. Try again later when he is in a better mood.

Quiet times at home can be ideal for heartwarming photos of your baby as he sleeps in his cot, plays with his brothers and sisters or watches you doing the chores. Expressions of concentration when your baby is spoon feeding, with a clasped fist around a spoon, can provide amusements.

These photos are lively and colourful and it is one time when the subject and props are all in the same locality, so you don't have to worry too much about composition. The most important point to remember for taking this type of photo is that you must get in quite close to your subject.

Babies are much more spontaneous and unaffected than adults. Take advantage of your baby's concentration in play to capture expressions of curiosity, laughter and joy. With toddlers the opportunities to photograph in-doors are great; older babies have a keen sense of humour.

One of the tricks which will coax your baby into making wonderful faces is to use puppets and songs. Otherwise, try tying a balloon to your camera, wear something colourful on your head.

Be prepared with the correct equipment but allow time to watch your baby's expressions without directing the changes. Take advantage of the natural light and keep the camera loaded with a versable film. A fast film will let you use the natural light through a windows behind your baby, so you won't have to use a flash. A medium telephoto lens and a fast film will also let you record your child's changing expressions from a distance. Always focus carefully when taking photos with a telephoto lens especially when the light levels are low.

It's important to frame close-up photos that give prominence to your baby's face and exposed features. Newborn babies will look tiny if you photograph them from too great a distance.

Photgraphing your baby outdoors will provide him with new visual interests and you may find new effects. By tilting your camera upwards you can show your baby against the clear blue sky or against a background of patterned leaves or branches.

Babies find water fascinating: pools, puddles, lakes, rivers and the ocean can enhance baby photographs. Remember that the reflective qualities of water can affect the mood or colour of your photos.

❑❑❑

Other Books on

HEALTH BOOKS

1. Child Development (New)	195/-
2. Yoga For Daily Life (New)	295/-
3. A Guide to Your Pregnancy (New)	175/-
4. Ayurveda for All (New)	175/-
5. A Guide to Migraine, Airthritis, Cervical Spondylosis, and Backache (New)	125/-
6. Body and Beauty Care (New)	125/-
7. Yoga for All (New)	250/-
8. Child Care and Nutrition	125/-
9. Naturopathy Modern Way of Life	125/-
10. First Aid How to Handle an Accident	125/-
11. Acupressure in Daily Life	125/-
12. Complete Book of Yoga	150/-
13. Look Younger at Any Age	125/-
14. HIV/AIDS - Transmission, Prevention & Alternative Therapies	110/-
15. Diabetics and Diet	110/-
16. Increase your Height & Loose your Weight	125/-
17. Make Fitness A Way of Life	195/-
18. Common Problems of Children	160/-
19. Handbook of Nutrition & Dietetics	250/-
20. A Guide to Massage Therapy	125/-
21. A Guide to Family Medicine	150/-
22. A Guide to Digestive Disorders	125/-
23. Complete Book of Child Care	150/-
24. A Guide to Homoeopathy	125/-
25. Life Begins at 40	125/-
26. Alternative Therapies	125/-
27. How to Overcome Stress	125/-
28. Yoga Therapy	250/-
29. Obesity	125/-
30. Self Motivation	125/-
31. Yoga for Health and Relaxation	160/-
32. Women Disorders and Pregnancy	125/-
33. A Guide to Body Pains	125/-
34. Sex Education	125/-
35. Common Diseases and Cure	125/-
36. Pranayama for Better Life	125/-
37. Herbal Home Remedies	125/-
38. A Guide to Beauty & Skin Care	125/-
39. A Guide to Heart Care	125/-
40. A Guide to High Blood Pressure	125/-
41. Cancer Causes and Prevention	125/-
42. Nature Cure for Common Diseases	125/-
43. Good Health Through Food and Regimen	110/-
44. A Guide to Allergies	125/-
45. A Guide to Aging	125/-
46. Ayurveda for Health & Beauty	125/-